Programming HTML5 Applications

Zachary Kessin

O'REILLY®

Beijing · Cambridge · Farnham · Köln · Sebastopol · Tokyo

Programming HTML5 Applications

by Zachary Kessin

Copyright © 2012 Zachary Kessin. All rights reserved.
Printed in the United States of America.

Published by O'Reilly Media, Inc., 1005 Gravenstein Highway North, Sebastopol, CA 95472.

O'Reilly books may be purchased for educational, business, or sales promotional use. Online editions are also available for most titles (*http://my.safaribooksonline.com*). For more information, contact our corporate/institutional sales department: (800) 998-9938 or *corporate@oreilly.com*.

Editors: Andy Oram and Simon St. Laurent	**Indexer:** Jay Marchand
Production Editor: Jasmine Perez	**Cover Designer:** Karen Montgomery
Copyeditor: Audrey Doyle	**Interior Designer:** David Futato
Proofreader: Kiel Van Horn	**Illustrator:** Robert Romano

November 2011:   First Edition.

Revision History for the First Edition:

2011-11-8   First release

See *http://oreilly.com/catalog/errata.csp?isbn=9781449399085* for release details.

Nutshell Handbook, the Nutshell Handbook logo, and the O'Reilly logo are registered trademarks of O'Reilly Media, Inc. *Programming HTML5 Applications*, the image of a European storm petrel, and related trade dress are trademarks of O'Reilly Media, Inc.

Many of the designations used by manufacturers and sellers to distinguish their products are claimed as trademarks. Where those designations appear in this book, and O'Reilly Media, Inc., was aware of a trademark claim, the designations have been printed in caps or initial caps.

While every precaution has been taken in the preparation of this book, the publisher and author assume no responsibility for errors or omissions, or for damages resulting from the use of the information contained herein.

ISBN: 978-1-449-39908-5

[LSI]

1320769131

Table of Contents

Preface

This book reflects the evolution of the Web. Less and less can programming be treated as a distinct activity shoehorned into web pages through scripts. Instead, HTML and JavaScript are now intertwined in producing an enchanting user experience. With this book, you can master the latest in this evolution.

How This Book Is Organized

The elements of this book are as follows:

Chapter 1, *The Web As Application Platform*
Introduces the reasons for programming on the new HTML5 platforms and what they offer to the JavaScript programmer

Chapter 2, *The Power of JavaScript*
Explains some powerful features of JavaScript you may not already know, and why you need to use them to exploit the HTML5 features and associated libraries covered in this book

Chapter 3, *Testing JavaScript Applications*
Shows how to create and use tests in the unique environment provided by JavaScript and browsers

Chapter 4, *Local Storage*
Describes the `localStorage` and `sessionStorage` objects that permit simple data caching in the browser

Chapter 5, *IndexedDB*
Shows the more powerful NoSQL database that supports local storage

Chapter 6, *Files*
Describes how to read and upload files from the user's system

Chapter 7, *Taking It Offline*
Describes the steps you must go through to permit a user to use your application when the device is disconnected from the Internet

Chapter 8, *Splitting Up Work Through Web Workers*
   Shows the multithreading capabilities of HTML5 and JavaScript

Chapter 9, *Web Sockets*
   Shows how to transfer data between the browser and server more efficiently by using web sockets

Chapter 10, *New Tags*
   Summarizes tags introduced in HTML5 that are of particular interest to the web programmer

Appendix, *JavaScript Tools You Should Know*
   Describes tools used in the book, and others that can make coding easier and more accurate

Conventions Used in This Book

The following typographical conventions are used in this book:

Italic
   Indicates new terms, URLs, email addresses, filenames, and file extensions

`Constant width`
   Used for program listings, as well as within paragraphs to refer to program elements such as variable or function names, databases, data types, environment variables, statements, and keywords

`Constant width bold`
   Shows commands or other text that should be typed literally by the user

`Constant width italic`
   Shows text that should be replaced with user-supplied values or by values determined by context

This icon signifies a tip, suggestion, or general note.

This icon indicates a warning or caution.

Using Code Examples

This book is here to help you get your job done. In general, you may use the code in this book in your programs and documentation. You do not need to contact us for permission unless you're reproducing a significant portion of the code. For example, writing a program that uses several chunks of code from this book does not require permission. Selling or distributing a CD-ROM of examples from O'Reilly books does require permission. Answering a question by citing this book and quoting example code does not require permission. Incorporating a significant amount of example code from this book into your product's documentation does require permission.

We appreciate, but do not require, attribution. An attribution usually includes the title, author, publisher, and ISBN. For example: "*Programming HTML5 Applications* by Zachary Kessin (O'Reilly). Copyright 2012 Zachary Kessin, 978-1-449-39908-5."

If you feel your use of code examples falls outside fair use or the permission given here, feel free to contact us at *permissions@oreilly.com*.

Safari® Books Online

Safari Books Online is an on-demand digital library that lets you easily search more than 7,500 technology and creative reference books and videos to find the answers you need quickly.

With a subscription, you can read any page and watch any video from our library online. Read books on your cell phone and mobile devices. Access new titles before they are available for print, and get exclusive access to manuscripts in development and post feedback for the authors. Copy and paste code samples, organize your favorites, download chapters, bookmark key sections, create notes, print out pages, and benefit from tons of other time-saving features.

O'Reilly Media has uploaded this book to the Safari Books Online service. To have full digital access to this book and others on similar topics from O'Reilly and other publishers, sign up for free at *http://my.safaribooksonline.com*.

How to Contact Us

Please address comments and questions concerning this book to the publisher:

O'Reilly Media, Inc.
1005 Gravenstein Highway North
Sebastopol, CA 95472
800-998-9938 (in the United States or Canada)
707-829-0515 (international or local)
707-829-0104 (fax)

We have a web page for this book, where we list errata, examples, and any additional information. You can access this page at:

http://shop.oreilly.com/product/0636920015116.do

To comment or ask technical questions about this book, send email to:

bookquestions@oreilly.com

For more information about our books, courses, conferences, and news, see our website at *http://www.oreilly.com*.

Find us on Facebook: *http://facebook.com/oreilly*

Follow us on Twitter: *http://twitter.com/oreillymedia*

Watch us on YouTube: *http://www.youtube.com/oreillymedia*

Acknowledgments

A book is a team effort, and I could not have written this book without a great team behind me. First of all, I must thank Simon St. Laurent for giving me the chance to write this book and supporting me through the process of putting it together. I must also thank Andy Oram for his editorial prowess and ability to make the book better. Also, thank you to my technical reviewers, Shelley Powers and Dionysios Synodinos, for great feedback.

I must also thank the Israeli developer community for existing: my former coworkers at Mytopia, who supported me in this project for more than a year, and the gang at Sayeret Lambda, which has become the place in Tel Aviv to talk about programming.

Finally, I would like to thank my wife, Devora, for all her support in this project. I could not have done it without you.

CHAPTER 1

The Web As Application Platform

HTML5 makes the Web a first-class environment for creating real applications. It reinforces JavaScript's existing tool set with key extensions to the browser APIs that make it easier to create applications that feel (and can be) complete in themselves, not just views on some distant server process.

The Web began as a way to share files, stored on a web server, that changed only occasionally. Developers quickly figured out how to generate those files on the fly, taking the first big step toward building applications. The next big step was adding interactivity in the browser client. JavaScript and the Document Object Model (DOM) let developers create Dynamic HTML, as the "browser wars" raged and then suddenly stopped. After a few years, Ajax brought these techniques back into style, adding some tools to let pages communicate with the server in smaller chunks.

HTML5 builds on these 20 years of development, and fills in some critical gaps. On the surface, many of HTML5's changes add support for features (especially multimedia and graphics) that had previously required plug-ins, but underneath, it gives JavaScript programmers the tools they need to create standalone (or at least more loosely tethered) applications using HTML for structure, CSS for presentation, and JavaScript for logic and behavior.

Adding Power to Web Applications

HTML5 raises the bar for web applications. While it still has to work under security constraints, it finally provides tools that desktop developers have expected for years:

Local data storage
>   It can store up to 5 MB of data, referenced with a key-value system.

Databases
>   Originally a SQLite-based API, the tide seems to have shifted to IndexedDB, a NoSQL system that is natively JavaScript.

Files

> While applications still can't freely access the filesystem (for obvious security reasons), they can now work with files the user specifies and are starting to be able to create files as well.

Taking it offline

> When a laptop or phone is in airplane mode, web applications are not able to communicate with the server. Manifest files help developers work around that by caching files for later use.

Web Workers

> Threads and forks have always been problematic, but JavaScript simply didn't offer them. Web Workers provide a way to put application processes into separate spaces where they can work without blocking other code.

Web sockets

> Hypertext Transfer Protocol (HTTP) has been the foundation of the Web, despite a few updates over time. Web sockets transform the request-response approach to create much more flexible communication systems.

There's much more, of course—from geolocation to audio and video to Canvas graphics to a wide variety of minor new tags—but these provide the foundations for building industrial-strength applications in HTML5.

Developing Web Applications

In the old days, a complex web application might be a catalog, which would be static pages derived from a database, or a JavaScript loan calculator. But no one would have dreamed of doing complex applications in JavaScript. Those required Java or maybe a dedicated client/server application written in C or C++. Indeed, in the days before the DOM and Ajax, developing complex applications in JavaScript would have been pretty much impossible. However, Ajax introduced the ability to interact with the server without reloading the page, and the DOM allowed the programmer to change HTML on the fly.

In 2007, Google introduced Gears, a browser extension that gave the developer a lot more power than had been there before. Gears allowed the browser to work offline, to enable users to store more data in the browser and have a worker pool to offload long-running tasks. Gears has since been discontinued, as most of its features have migrated into HTML5 in modified forms.

The modern Web features a full range of sites, from things that are still effectively old-style collections of documents, like Wikipedia, to sites that offer interactions with other people, such as Facebook, YouTube, and eBay, to things that can serve as replacements for desktop applications, such as Gmail and Google Docs. Many formerly standalone applications, such as mail clients, have become part and parcel of the web experience.

In the modern Web, the line between applications and pages has blurred. The difference at this point is only in the intent of the site.

Running an application in the browser has some major advantages for both the user and the developer. For the user, there is no commitment to the application: you try it out, and if you don't like it, you can move on to the next page with nothing left behind to clutter up your disk. Trying new applications is also reasonably safe, in that they run in a sandboxed environment. New versions of the application are automatically downloaded to the browser when the developer updates the code. Web applications rarely have version numbers, at least public ones.

For the developer, the case is even stronger. First of all, the things that are an advantage to the users are also good for the developers. There is no installation program to write, and new versions can automatically be sent to the users, making small, incremental updates not only possible but practical. However, there are other bonuses as well.

The Web is cross-platform. It is possible to write a web page that will work on Windows XP, Windows Vista, Windows 7, Mac OS X, Linux, the iPhone/iPad, and Android. Doing that with a conventional development tool would be a monumental task. But with the Web and some forethought it almost comes for free. A web application built on standards with a library like jQuery will be able to run on major browsers on all those platforms and a few others. While at one point Sun hoped that its Java applets would define the Web as a platform, JavaScript has turned out to become the default web platform.

You can even run web applications on mobile devices, at least the ones that today are called smartphones. With a wrapper like PhoneGap, you can create an HTML5 app and package it for sale in the App Store, the Android Market, and more. You might create an application that interacts heavily with a web server, or you might create a completely self-contained application. Both options are available.

The real place that the Web, prior to HTML5, traditionally falls short is that a web application, running on a computer with gigabytes of memory and disk space, acts almost like it is running on an old VT320 terminal. All data storage must be done on a server, all files must be loaded from the server, and every interaction pretty much requires a round-trip to the server. This can cause the user experience to feel slow, especially if the server is far away from the user. If every time the user wishes to look up something there is a minimum response time of 400 milliseconds before any actions can be taken, the application will feel slow. From my office in Tel Aviv to a server in California, the round-trip time for an ICMP ping is about 250 ms. Any action on the server would be extra and slow that down even more. Mobile device communications can, of course, be even slower.

JavaScript's Triumph

Though JavaScript has been a key component of web development since it first appeared in 1995, it spent a decade or so with a bad reputation. It offered weak performance, was saddled with a quirky syntax that led to mysterious bugs, and suffered from its dependence on the DOM. Browsers kept it locked in a "sandbox," easing users' security concerns but making it very difficult for developers to provide features that seemed trivial in more traditional desktop application development.

Scripting culture created its own problems. Although providing a very low barrier to entry is a good thing, it does come with costs. One of those costs is that such a language often allows inexperienced programmers to do some very ill-advised things. Beginning programmers could easily find JavaScript examples on the Web, cut and paste them, change a few things, and have something that mostly worked. Unfortunately, maintaining such code becomes more and more difficult over time.

With the Ajax revival, developers took a new look at JavaScript. Some have worked on improving the engines interpreting and running JavaScript code, leading to substantial speed improvements. Others focused on the language itself, realizing that it had some very nice features, and consequently developing best practices like those outlined in *JavaScript: The Good Parts* by Douglas Crockford (O'Reilly, 2008).

Beyond the core language, developers built tools that made debugging JavaScript much easier. Although Venkman, an early debugger, had appeared in 1998, the 2006 release of Firebug became the gold standard of JavaScript debuggers. It allows the developer to track Ajax calls, view the state of the DOM and CSS, single-step through code, and much more. Browsers built on WebKit, notably Apple's Safari and Google Chrome, offer similar functionality built in, and Opera Dragonfly provides support for Opera. Even developers working in the confined spaces of mobile devices can now get Firebug-like debugging with weinre (WEb INspector REmote).

The final key component in this massive recent investment in JavaScript was libraries. Developers still might not understand all the code they were using, but organizing that code into readily upgradeable and sometimes even interchangeable libraries simplified code management.

jQuery

> If anything can be described as the gold standard of JavaScript libraries, it would have to be John Resig's jQuery library, which forms a wrapper around the DOM and other JavaScript objects such as the `XMLHttpRequest` object, and makes doing all sorts of things in JavaScript a lot easier and a lot more fun. In many ways, jQuery is the essential JavaScript library that every JavaScript programmer should know.
>
> To learn jQuery, see the jQuery website (*http://jquery.org*) or a number of good books on the subject, such as *Head First jQuery* by Ryan Benedetti and Ronan Cranley or *jQuery Cookbook* by Cody Lindley, both published by O'Reilly. Many examples in this book are written using jQuery.

ExtJS

Whereas jQuery forms a wrapper around the DOM, Sencha's (*http://sencha.com*) ExtJS tries to abstract it away as much as possible. ExtJS features a rich widget set that can live in a web page and provide many of the widgets, such as trees, grids, forms, buttons, and so on, that desktop developers are familar with. The entire system is very well thought out, fits together well, and makes developing many kinds of applications a joy. Although the ExtJS library takes up a lot of space, the expenditure is worthwhile for some kinds of application development.

One nice feature of ExtJS is that many of its objects know how to save their state. So if a user takes a grid and reorganizes the columns, the state can be saved so that the same order appears the next time the user views that grid. "Using localStorage in ExtJS" on page 53 will show how to use the HTML5 `localStorage` facility with this feature.

Google Web Toolkit, etc.

Tools such as GWT allow the programmer to write Java code, which is then compiled down to JavaScript and can be run on the browser.

CHAPTER 2

The Power of JavaScript

Although JavaScript is not a difficult language to program, it can be challenging to rise to the level of a true expert. There are several key factors to becoming a skilled JavaScript programmer. The techniques in this chapter will appear repeatedly in the libraries and programming practices taught in the rest of this book, so you should familiarize yourself with these techniques before continuing with those chapters.

There are a number of excellent tools for JavaScript programming, some of them listed in the Appendix. These tools can provide you with a lot of assistance. Specifically, JSLint will catch a large number of errors that a programmer might miss. Sites such as StackOverflow (*http://stackoverflow.com/*) and O'Reilly Answers (*http://answers.oreilly .com*) will be a good source of other tools.

This chapter is not a full introduction to the power of JavaScript. O'Reilly publishes a number of excellent books on Javscript, including:

- *JavaScript, The Good Parts* by Douglas Crockford
- *JavaScript: The Definitive Guide* by David Flanagan
- *High Performance JavaScript* by Nicholas C. Zakas
- *JavaScript Patterns* by Stoyan Stefanov

Nonblocking I/O and Callbacks

The first key to JavaScript, after learning the language itself, is to understand event-driven programming. In the environment where JavaScript runs, operations tend to be asynchronous, which is to say that they are set up in one place and will execute later after some external event happens.

This can represent a major change from the way I/O happens in traditional languages. Take Example 2-1 as a typical case of I/O in a traditional language, in this case PHP. The line $db->getAll($query); requires the database to access the disk, and therefore will take orders of magnitude more time to run than the rest of the function. While the program is waiting for the server to execute, the query statement is blocked and the program is doing nothing. In a server-side language like PHP, where there can be many parallel threads or processes of execution, this isn't usually a problem.

Example 2-1. Blocking I/O in PHP

```
function getFromDatabase()
{
  $db = getDatabase();
  $query = "SELECT name FROM countries";
  $result = $db->getAll($query);
  return $result;
}
```

In JavaScript, however, there is only one thread of execution, so if the function is blocked, nothing else happens and the user interface is frozen. Therefore, JavaScript must find a different way to handle I/O (including all network operations). What Java-Script does is return right away from a method that might be perceived as slow, leaving behind a function that gets called when the operation (say, downloading new data from the web server) is complete. The function is known as a *callback*. When making an Ajax call to the server, the JavaScript launches the request and then goes on to do something else. It provides a function that is called when the server call is finished. This function is called (hence the term *callback*) with the data that is returned from the server at the time when the data is ready.

As an analogy, consider two ways of buying an item at a grocery store. Some stores leave items behind the counter, so you have to ask a salesperson for the item and wait while she retrieves it. That's like the PHP program just shown. Other stores have a deli counter where you can request an order and get a number. You can go off to do other shopping, and when your order is ready, you can pick it up. That situation is like a callback.

In general, a fast operation can be blocking, because it should return the data requested right away. A slow operation, such as a call to a server that may take several seconds, should be nonblocking and should return its data via a callback function. The presence of a callback option in a function will provide a good clue to the relative time it will take for an operation to run. In a single-threaded language like JavaScript, a function can't block while waiting for the network or user without locking up the browser.

So a major step to JavaScript mastery involves using callbacks strategically and knowing when they'll be triggered. When you use a `DataStore` object with Ajax, for example, the data will not be there for a second or two. Using a closure to create a callback is the correct way to handle data loading (see "Closures" on page 11). All such external I/O (e.g., databases, calls to the server) should be nonblocking in JavaScript, so learning to use closures and callbacks is critical.

With a few exceptions that should probably be avoided, JavaScript I/O does not block. The three major exceptions to this rule are the window methods `alert()`, `confirm()`, and `prompt()`. These three methods do, in fact, block all JavaScript on the page from the moment when they are called to the moment when the user dismisses the dialog. In addition, the XHR object can make an Ajax call to the server in asynchronous mode. This can be used safely in a Web Worker, but in the main window it will cause the browser UI to lock up, so it should be avoided there.

Lambda Functions Are Powerful

Programmers who have come to JavaScript from PHP or other procedural languages will tend to treat JavaScript functions like those in the languages that they have already used. While it is possible to use JavaScript functions in this way, it is missing a large chunk of what makes JavaScript functions so powerful.

JavaScript functions can be created with the function statement (Example 2-2) or the function expression (Example 2-3). These two forms look pretty similar, and both examples produce a function called `square` that will square a number. However, there are some key differences. The first form is subject to *hoisting*, which is to say that the function will be created at the start of the enclosing scope. So you can't use a function statement when you want the function defined conditionally, because JavaScript won't wait for the conditional statement to be executed before deciding whether to create the function. In practice, most browsers allow you to put a function inside an `if`, but it is not a good idea, as what browsers will do in this case can vary. It is much better to use a function statement if the definition of a function should be conditional.

Example 2-2. Function statement

```
function square(x) {
    return x * x;
} // Note lack of a ;
```

Example 2-3. Function expression

```
var square = function(x) {
    return x * x;
};
```

In the second form, the function expression, the function is created when execution gets to that point in the flow of the program. It is possible to define a function conditionally, or to have the function defined inside a larger statement.

The function expression, in addition, assigns no name to the function, so the function can be left anonymous. However, the example shown assigns a name (`square`) on the left side of the equals sign, which is a good idea for two reasons. First, when you are debugging a program, assigning a name allows you to tell which function you're seeing in a stack trace; without it, the function will show up as anonymous. It can be quite frustrating to look at a stack trace in Firebug and see a stack of nine or ten functions, all of which are simply listed as anonymous. Also, assigning a function name allows you to call the function recursively if desired.

A function expression can be used anywhere in JavaScript that an expression can appear. So a function can be assigned to a variable as in Example 2-3, but it can also be assigned to an object member or passed to a function.

JavaScript functions are more like the Lisp lambdas than C functions. In C-type languages (including Java and C++), a function is basically a static thing. It is not an object on which you can operate. While you can pass objects as arguments to functions, there is little ability to build composite objects or otherwise expand objects.

 Back in the 1950s when Lisp was first being created, the folks at MIT were being heavily influenced by Alonzo Church's Lambda Calculus, which provided a mathematical framework for dealing with functions and recursion. So John McCarthy used the keyword lambda for dealing with an anonymous function. This has propagated to other languages such as Perl, Python, and Ruby. Although the keyword lambda does not appear in JavaScript, its functions do the same things.

As in Lisp, functions in JavaScript are first-class citizens of the language. A function in JavaScript is just data with a special property that can be executed. But like all other variables in JavaScript, a function can be operated on. In C and similar languages, functions and data are in effect two separate spaces. In JavaScript, functions are data and can be used in every place that you can use data. A function can be assigned to a variable, passed as a parameter, or returned by a function. Passing a function to another function is a very common operation in JavaScript. For example, this would be used when creating a callback for a button click (see Example 2-4). Also, a function can be changed by simple assignment.

Example 2-4. ExtJS Button with function as handler

```
var button = new Ext.Button({
    text: 'Save',
    handler: function() {
        // Do Save here
    }
});
```

Closures

Access to functions as first-class objects in JavaScript would not be worth as much, were it not for the property that goes along with it called *closure*. Closure is yet another element from Lisp that has migrated into JavaScript. When a function is created in JavaScript, the function has access to any lexically scoped variables that were in the environment that created it. Those variables are still available even if the context in which they were originally defined has finished executing. The variables may be accessed and modified by the inner function as well as the outer function.

Closures are often useful for constructing callbacks. A closure should be used whenever a second function will run as a response to some event but needs to know what has happened before.

This is often useful when building a function generator, as each time the generator function runs it will have a different outer state, which will be encapsulated with the created function. It is also possible to create more than one function in a generator, all of which are closed onto the same environment.

Closures are one of the most powerful features in JavaScript. In a simple case, a closure can be used to create functions that can access the variables of an outer scope to allow callbacks to access data from the controlling function. However, even more powerful is the ability to create custom functions that bind variables into a scope.

In Example 2-5, a DOM element or CSS selector called el is wrapped in a function to allow the HTML content to be set with a simple function call. The outer function (factory) binds the element el to a lexical variable that is used by the inner function to set the element via jQuery. The outer function returns the inner function as its return value. The result of the example is to set the variable updateElement to the inner set function, with el already bound to a CSS selector. When a program calls factory with a CSS selector, it returns a function that can be used to set the HTML of the relevant HTML element.

Example 2-5. Basic closure

```
var factory = function factory (el)
    {
        return function set(html)
        {
            $(el).html(html);
        };
    };
```

It is also possible to create several functions that are closed on one scope. If a function returns several functions in an object or array, all of those functions will have access to the internal variables of the creating function.

Example 2-6 adds to the browser's toolbar the buttons defined in the `tools` array. Each of the buttons gets its own handler, named `clickHandler`. This function has access to the calling function's variables, and embeds the `button` and `tool` variables into its operations. You can easily update the application by adding or subtracting an element from the `tools` array, and the button with all the defined functionality will appear or disappear.

Example 2-6. Closure in a button

```
$('document').ready(function Ready() {
    var button, tools;
    tools = ['save', 'add', 'delete'];
    console.info($('div#toolbar'));
    tools.forEach(function (tool) {
        console.info(tool);
        var button = $('<button>').text(tool).attr({
            css: 'tool'
        }).appendTo('div#toolbar');
        button.click(function clickHandler() {
            console.info(tool, button);
            alert("User clicked " + tool);
        });
    });

});
```

When using closures, it can be hard to know which variables are or are not in the scope of a function. However, both Google Chrome's DevTools and Firebug will show the list of closed variables.

In Firebug, the scope chain can be seen in the Script tab by looking under "Watch." Under all the variables of the current scope will be a ladder of the scopes going up to the main "window" object.

In DevTools, for example, when the code is halted in the debugger, a subsection called "closure" in the right-hand column under Scope Variables will show the closed variables for the current function (see Figure 2-1). In this case, it shows that we have clicked on the "delete" button and lists the reference to the jQuery object for the button itself.

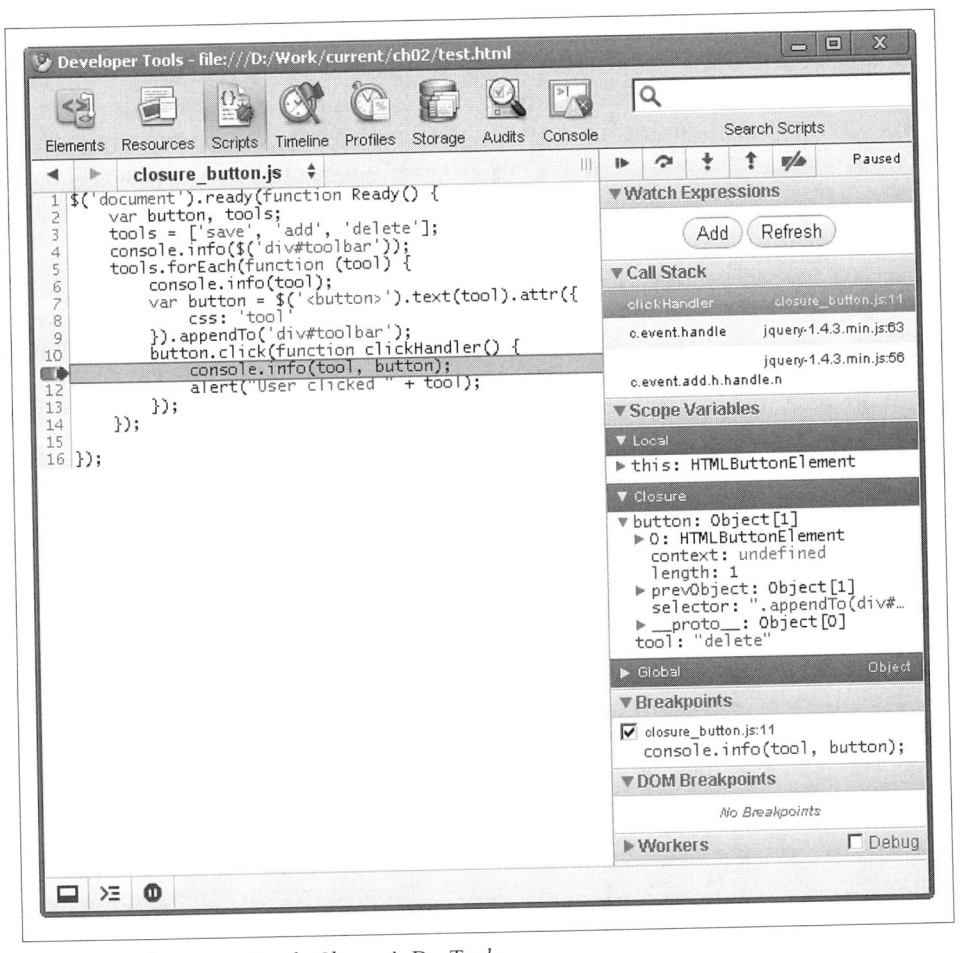

Figure 2-1. Closures in Google Chrome's DevTools

Functional Programming

Functional programming is a methodology that is more commonly associated with languages like Lisp, Scala, Erlang, F#, or Haskell, but works quite well in JavaScript also. Functional programming rests on a couple basic assumptions:

- Functions are first-class citizens of the language and can be used where any other value can be used.
- Complex behavior can be built by composition of simple functions.
- Functions return values. In many cases, a given function will always return the same value for the same inputs.

In mathematics, functions do not have side effects. Take a classical mathematical function like `y = sin(x)`. It just returns a value that `y` can store, but does not change `x` or anything in the global state of the program. By ensuring that functions are "pure" (have no side effects), this practice enables the function to be called from anywhere in the program without causing something strange to happen. The problem with side effects in programming is that they can cause strange dependencies that can be very hard to track down. If calling a method can cause data to be corrupted somewhere else, it greatly increases the potential for bugs that will be very difficult to find.

JavaScript functions can have side effects, and there is no built-in way to prevent functions from having side effects. In addition, JavaScript functions do not by default return values unless the `return` statement has been explicitly invoked to return a value. In the absence of a `return` statement, the function will return `undefined`.

When employing functional programming, the programmer often falls into the pattern of using many very small functions, often with only two or three lines of code each, to accomplish a goal. This can be a very good design technique, as very short functions are, in general, easier to make correct and easier to test.

It is often the case that complex behavior can be built up from simple functions by composition. A chain of functions can be built up from simple functions, in which each function returns `this`, allowing the next function to be called. The last function in the chain can return `this`.

The jQuery library often uses function changes such as in Example 2-7. In this example, jQuery finds a DOM item, sets its text, fades it into view, and then sets a click handler on it that will hide it with a second DOM chain.

Example 2-7. Chaining functions with a closure

```
$('div.alert').text("Message").fadein
 (2000).click(
 function ()
  {
    $(this).fadeout(2000);
  }
);
```

One very powerful pattern of functional programming is the *higher-order function*. A higher-order function takes a function as an argument to abstract out specific behavior while leaving the generic behavior in the outer function.

A good example of a higher-order function is the **Array** map function (see "Array Iteration Operations" on page 22). It takes an array and returns a new array that is the result of applying the passed function to each element in the array. This model can be applied to a wide range of circumstances beyond just array manipulation. As a general pattern, the higher-order function can be used wherever a generic behavior needs a few specific modifications.

The jQuery library's interface tends to favor functional programming. This interface is particularly apt for selecting a set of DOM nodes from the page and then providing a functional interface to interact with those nodes.

In addition, most of the methods of jQuery return a value so that they can be chained. For example, to find all the images wider than a set size in a page, one could select all the images in the page, filter out all those that are smaller than 300 pixels, and then scale all those that are left in the list.

Example 2-8 does exactly that. It selects all the images in a document (anything with an img tag), uses the `filter` function to determine which ones have a width greater than 300 pixels (maxWidth), and scales those. By making the filter and scale functions very simple, you can be more confident that the code will work as intended.

Example 2-8. Scaling images

```
var scaleImages = (function (maxWidth)
{
  return function ()
  {
    $('img').filter(function ()
    {
      return $(this).width() > maxWidth;
    }).each(function ()
    {
      $(this).width(maxWidth);
    });
  };
}(300));
```

When processing a list of operations in a time-consuming procedure, such as in an Ajax call, it is sometimes not practical to send the entire list to the server in one request. For example, it may be that sending the entire list will cause the server to time out.

In this case, to iterate over the list, it is useful to think of the list as a head and tail. Take the first element off the list (or the first few elements) and process that, then process the rest of the list by use of recursion until the list is empty (see Example 2-9).

I have used this strategy when adding data to a REST interface. Each call to the interface takes on average about one second, so it is not practical to call it 500 times from one Ajax call. In this case, I was able to process the list by recursion.

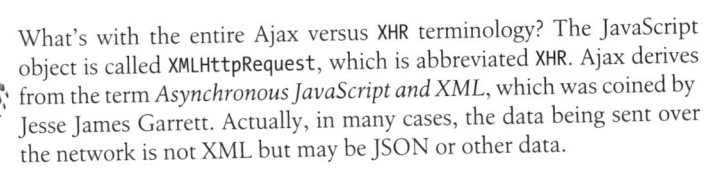 What's with the entire Ajax versus XHR terminology? The JavaScript object is called XMLHttpRequest, which is abbreviated XHR. Ajax derives from the term *Asynchronous JavaScript and XML*, which was coined by Jesse James Garrett. Actually, in many cases, the data being sent over the network is not XML but may be JSON or other data.

Example 2-9. List recursion

```
function iterateAjax(tasks) {
    function iterator(tasks) {
        $.ajax({
            url: 'index.php',
            data: tasks[0],
            success: function(data, status, XMLHttpRequest) {
                if (tasks.length > 0) {
                    // Do something with the results here
                    iterator(tasks.slice(1));
                }
            }
        });
    }
    iterator(tasks);
}
```

Although building an entire single-page web application with only functional programming styles would not be practical, functional programming still provides many useful ideas that should not be ignored. Functional programming is very well suited, for instance, for use with Web Workers (see Chapter 8).

Not a lot has been written about functional programming in JavaScript, but there is quite a lot in other languages that can be applied to JavaScript. For more on functional programming, see these books:

- *Real World Haskell* by Bryan O'Sullivan, John Goerzen, and Donald Bruce Stewart (O'Reilly)
- *Programming Scala* by Dean Wampler and Alex Payne (O'Reilly)
- *Structure and Interpretation of Computer Programs* by Harold Abelson and Gerald Jay Sussman (MIT Press)

Prototypes and How to Expand Objects

Everything in JavaScript can have methods attached to it. Every element has some basic methods that can be used by the programmer to enhance its usefulness. JavaScript primitives such as Booleans, strings, and numbers have a second life as objects. The transformation from primitive to object is transparent, so it is possible to apply these methods to a primitive. Actually, what happens is that a simple value—for example, a string—will be converted to an object, and then converted back if needed.

Strings offer a large number of methods that can be called to manipulate them. A few will modify the string in place, but most will return a new string. A full list can be found on the Mozilla Developer Network website (*https://developer.mozilla.org/en/javascript*), but here are a few highlights:

```
string.indexOf()
```
    Returns the first index of a substring in a string, or −1 if not found

```
string.lastIndexOf()
```
Same as `indexOf()`, but starting at the end

```
string.match()
```
Matches a regular expression in a string

```
string.replace()
```
Replaces a regular expression (specified as a function or string) with a new string

```
string.split()
```
Splits a string into an array of substrings

```
string.slice()
```
Extracts a substring

However, there may come a time when the predefined methods are not enough and some custom functionality is required. In this case, JavaScript provides an unusual and very powerful feature, a way to extend a built-in object. Although you can always assign a method to a JavaScript object with a simple assignment, that is not always the best way to do it. If you want to add a method to every string, you can attach a method to the `String.prototype` object. In the JavaScript object system, each object inherits from a chain of prototypes, so by adding methods somewhere in that chain you can add to an entire type of object.

Here is an example to illustrate the concept. The goal is to create a new method named `populate` that substitutes values into a template. The template is the object on which the method is called, for instance:

```
Hello {name}
```

The string should contain keywords in curly braces that the programmer wants to replace with specific values. The parameter to `populate` is an object specifying keywords in the template and values to substitute. Thus, if the argument contains a property called `name`, the value for `name` is plugged in to the string.

Once the code in Example 2-10 is run, the `populate` method is attached to all strings. When `populate` is called, it refers to the string on which it is called through the standard JavaScript object `this`. Having the value of `this`, the `populate` method can use simple substitution to plug in values from its parameter. In general, it is a good idea to not modify the object on which a method is called, but to return a new instance of the object (an idea from functional programming).

Example 2-10. String token replacement

```
String.prototype.populate = function populate(params) {
    var str = this.replace(/\{\w+\}/g, function stringFormatInner(word) {
        return params[word.substr(1, word.length - 2)];
    });
    return str;
};

$('.target').html("Hello {name}".populate({
```

```
    name: "Zach"
}));
```

Of course, strings are not the only types of objects in JavaScript that have prototypes. Numbers, arrays, objects, Booleans, and functions do as well.

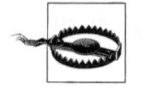 Extending the prototypes of basic objects such as Object, Array, and so on, can sometimes break libraries. The culprit is usually creating a property that already existed on the object. Be sure that the property you are creating does not exist before adding it, and test carefully.

In truth, extending base types in JavaScript is a practice that attracts a lot of debate. Some people say it should never be done. I think it is such a powerful tool that it cannot be ruled out completely.

The Number prototype works exactly the same way as the one for strings. So it is very possible to define a new method to take care of any need that may be required. If, for example, an application requires squaring numbers on a regular basis, it would be easy to add the method, as shown in Example 2-11.

Example 2-11. Using Number.prototype

```
Number.prototype.square = function square() {
    return this * this;
};
6.square(); // 36
```

Expanding Functions with Prototypes

In addition to data objects such as strings and arrays, functions also have a prototype. This can be used to create composite functions that are very powerful. By combining simple functions into larger units, using the Function.prototype to add methods to the Function object, you can pull apart complex logic into much simpler cases. In fact, many toolkits do exactly this and provide some methods to accomplish some of these tasks.

One example of prototyping, which may increase the robustness of your code throughout its execution, is to add error-checking before executing a function. In the code in Example 2-12, a cube function runs without checking that its input is a number. The code wraps the function in an interceptor that does the check. Whenever cube is subsequently called, the interceptor runs first, then calls the original cube if the input is a number.

Example 2-12. Function interceptor

```
Function.prototype.createInterceptor = function createInterceptor(fn) {
    var scope = {};
    return function() {
        if (fn.apply(scope, arguments)) {
```

```
            return this.apply(scope, arguments);
        }
        else {
            return null;
        }
    };
};

var interceptMe = function cube(x) {
    console.info(x);
    return Math.pow(x, 3);
};

var cube = interceptMe.createInterceptor(function(x) {
    return typeof x === "number";
});
```

As a more extensive example, say that you wish to regularly compute Fibonacci sequences. A very simple brute force approach would be something like Example 2-13. However, something as trivial as fib(40) would take quite a long time to run.

Example 2-13. Basic Fibonacci calculation

```
var fib = function fib(n) {
    if (n === 1 || n === 2) {
        return 1;
    }
    return (fib(n - 1) + fib(n - 2));
};
```

A quick trace through a sample run of this function shows that it does a lot of redundant calculations. It would be much faster to have a Fibonacci method that could calculate each value only once. We can do this by wrapping the Fibonacci function with an interceptor method that caches the result of each iteration (see Example 2-14). The interceptor does not need to know anything about how a Fibonacci sequence is generated; it just has to know that for a given input, it should always produce the same output. So once fib(n) is computed, it becomes a simple matter of doing a lookup, and if it is not known, it can be computed.

Example 2-14 has two parts: the cache method and the actual Fibonacci sequence generator. The cache method does not know anything about this sequence except for one fact: that any given input value will always return the same value, which can be cached. Thus, when decoratedFib(32) is called, the cache will first check whether it has already computed the result for 32. If it has, it will just return it. If it has not, it will start to compute it. But the Fibonacci sequence is heavily recursive. So to compute the Fibonacci sequence for 32, the function first must compute it for 31, and so on. The function will recursively look for a solution until it hits a value it has. If this is the first time running the function, it will find n = 2 and n = 1, which are in the seed values.

Although the Fibonacci sequence is not something many people spend much time on, it is a good example of how using a function prototype can take two very short functions and combine them for a very powerful result.

 This example is more complex than it really has to be in order to show how to cache function results from functions that have no side effects. But this is probably not the best way to write this code.

Example 2-14. Advanced Fibonacci calculation

```
var smartFib = (function makeFib() {
    var fibsequence = [0, 1, 1];
    var fib = function fib(n) {
        if (fibsequence[n]) {
            return fibsequence[n];
        }
        fibN = fib(n - 1) + fib(n - 2);
        fibsequence[n] = fibN;
        return fibsequence[n];
    };
    return fib;
}());

Function.prototype.decorate = function Decorate(params) {
    return params.decorator(this, params.initialData);
};

var cache = function cache(lambda, initial) {
    return function cacheRunner(n) {
        if (initial[n] !== undefined) {
            return initial[n];
        }
        else {
            initial[n] = lambda(n);
            return initial[n];
        }
    };
};

var decoratedFib = function fib(n) {
    return decoratedFib(n - 1) + decoratedFib(n - 2);
}.decorate({
    decorator: cache,
    initialData: [0, 1, 1]
});
```

Suppose you have a function that should run periodically in response to user inputs but should not run more than once in a given time period. It would be simple using the Function prototype to create a wrapper function that would store when that function was last called and keep it from running if it is called again within the designated time.

You could just quietly choose to not run it, or to throw an exception, as needed by the application.

On the flip side, it is also possible to create a method to a function that will cause it to execute after a delay, or periodically. Often, a task needs to run after an event but should not run too often. For instance, you might want to check on what a user is typing, but running the check after every keystroke would be excessive. Setting up a method that will run only once every 250 ms would make sense.

There are two approaches to this. First, you could run the method once and not allow it to run again until the required time has passed. Or you could create a method that will run at some time interval after it is called, and will reset the timer when called. This pattern is useful if the objective is to have something run when the user stops typing or when some other set of events pauses. In practice, a new method would act as a wrapper around the basic JavaScript `setTimeout()` and `setInterval()` methods, but make their use more convenient. It is also possible to create a method that will schedule a future task and cancel an existing task if it has already been scheduled.

Currying and Object Parameters

In functional programming, one common programming model is *currying* a function. Named for a feature of Haskell, currying refers to the practice of combining several parameters into a single object so that you can pass them to a function as a single parameter. If a function needs to take a large number of parameters, it is often best in JavaScript to forgo the long parameter list and take a single object as a parameter. By using an object as the parameter, you can turn all the various options into name/value pairs. One benefit of doing so is that the ordering of arguments becomes irrelevant. Furthermore, you can make some or all of the parameters optional. For complex methods accepting many options, this can be a great help. In particular, it is often useful for some of the object creation methods in ExtJS.

The easiest way to curry parameters is to create a function that takes a parameter block and returns a function that will call the original function with the presupplied parameters as defaults (see Example 2-15). This way, you can establish a set of defaults that you don't have to specify each time, while allowing callers to change any parameters they want.

Example 2-15. Curry example

```
Function.prototype.curry = function FunctionCurry(defaults) {
    var fn = this;
    return function(params) {
        return fn.apply(this, defaults.concat(params));
    };

};
```

This pattern can also be applied to object creation. For an object constructor that takes a parameter block, it is possible to subclass the object with a custom class that calls the parent constructor with a set of default parameters overlaid onto what the user passed.

Array Iteration Operations

Like other first-class objects in JavaScript, arrays also have methods. The standard array has a number of methods for the programmer. In the more recent versions of Firefox (later than version 1.5), a number of standard iteration methods have also been created.

The basic idea of these operations is that you take a lambda function and apply it to each element of an array to produce some result. Using this approach with a few smaller functions allows you to take an array and create a set of operations on it that can build an algebra of arrays. This in turn lets you build up a very robust set of operations from a basic set of operations.

The first of the array methods is map(), which takes an array and a method as arguments. It then applies the method to each element of the array and creates a new array from the return values. So given an array of numbers, it would be possible to create an array of squares of each number by simply applying a square function in map().

 The array methods such as map() are available on most modern browsers (e.g., they were added to Internet Explorer in version 9). However, if they are not available, they can be added. Sample code for all of the array methods can be found on the Mozilla Developer Network website.

The called function receives as parameters the current value of the array, the index of the current position in the array, and the entire array. Usually, the map worker function will only need to look at the current value of the array, as in Example 2-16.

Example 2-16. Array map

```
[1, 2, 3, 4 , 5].map(function (x){
    return x* x;
});
//Result:  [1,4,9,16,25]
```

However, there are a few cases where that may not be enough. In Example 2-17, the desire is to show a running average of the values in an array, so each element needs to know about its neighbors.

Example 2-17. Running average

```
function makeRunningAverage(list, size)
{
  return list.map(function (current, index, list)
  {
    var start, end, win;
```

```
    /* find start and end points of the rolling average window */
    start = index - size < 0 ?
        0 :
        index - size;
    /* extract that window */
    end = index + size > list.length ?
        list.length :
        index + size;
    win = list.slice(start, end); /* take an average */
    return win.reduce(function (accumulator, current)
    {
        return accumulator + current;
    }, 0) / (end - start);
  });
}
```

There are a few big advantages to using array elements this way instead of using a for loop. First, it is logically clean and isolates the iteration code, allowing the programmer to think of the array as a whole. Second, by avoiding side effects in the inner function and by keeping the functions short, you can write very robust code.

Another case that should be considered is when adding callback handlers. If you were to use a for loop to iterate over items and add handlers, you could not use the closure property of JavaScript functions. You might be tempted to use something like the code shown in Example 2-18. However, this will not do what you expect. In this case, the method will always show the last element. What is deceptive is that here, the value of i that is referenced in all cases is the final value. A closure will always see the current value of a variable, not the value when the closure was created. The for loop changes the value of i as it iterates over the list. In Example 2-19, the code will work correctly. In this case, the node referenced in each iteration is independent because it is inside the scope of the function.

Example 2-18. Loop with for

```
for (var i = 0; i < nodes.length; i += 1) {
    nodes[i].bind('click', function() {
        console.info(nodes[i]);
    });
}
```

Example 2-19. Binding with forEach

```
nodes.forEach(function(node) {
    node.bind('click', function() {
        console.info(node);
    });
});
```

The next method of note is filter(). This method takes an array and returns the subset of the array for which the method returns true. The iterator function shown in Example 2-20 receives the same parameters as it does for map(), but should return a boolean value.

Example 2-20. Filter function

```
[1,2,3,4,5].filter(even); => [2,4]
```

If you wish to know whether some fact is true for all elements of an array, use every(). It will apply a method to an array and return true if the method returns true for all elements in the array. It will stop after the first false.

If you wish to know whether some condition is true for *at least one* element of the list, use the some() method. This will return true if at least one element of a list returns true. Like every(), it will evaluate only enough elements to get a result.

The last two operators in the JavaScript algebra of arrays are reduce() and reduce Right(). The first method takes an array and reduces it to some single value. It is useful as an accumulator. In this case, the calling function also receives the accumulated value. So the code for using reduce() to sum up a list would look like Example 2-21. You can provide an optional initial value, which will be passed as the previous value on the first iteration. If you do not, it will start by using the first two elements of the array.

Example 2-21. Reduce function

```
[0,1,2,3,4,5].reduce(function(prev, current){
                     return prev + current;
                   },
                   initialValue);
```

If the JavaScript array algebra does not provide the method you need for a task, use the Array.prototype object to create it. If you have a list of numbers and you need to create a standard deviation from that list, for instance, you can simply apply a standard deviation method. In Example 2-22, a standard deviation method is added to the array prototype.

Example 2-22. Standard deviation

```
    var stdDev = [1,2,7,2....].stddev();
Array.reduce.sum = function sum() {
    var sum = this.reduce(function(previous, current) {
        return previous + current;
    });
    return sum;
};

Array.prototype.square = function squareArray() {
    return this.map(function(x) {
        return x * x;
    });
};

Array.prototype.mean = function mean() {
    return this.sum() / this.length;
};

Array.prototype.standardDeviation = function standardDeviation() {
```

```
    var mean = this.mean();
    var int1 = this.map(function(n) {
        return n - mean;
    });
    var int2 = int1.square();
    var int3 = Math.sqrt(int2.sum() / mean.length);
};

//Give it a shorter name
Array.prototype.stddev = Array.prototype.standardDeviation;
```

You Can Extend Objects, Too

If you like the map function in arrays and wish you had that for objects as well, there
is no reason why you could not add it. It is possible to build a map function that will
not only visit all the nodes of a JavaScript object, but also recursively apply a function
to each of its subnodes. This can be very useful for turning a data structure into some
form of a node tree. Example 2-23 checks to see whether the user's browser has already
defined map() and filter() for the object being assigned to, and then defines the
functions if necessary.

Example 2-23. Extending map and filter to objects

```
if (Object.prototype.map === undefined) {
    Object.prototype.map = function(fn) {
        var newObj = {};
        for (var i in this) {
            if (this.hasOwnProperty(i)) {
                newObj[i] = fn(i, this[i], this);
            }
        }
        return newObj;
    };
}

if (Object.prototype.filter === undefined) {
    Object.prototype.filter = function(fn) {
        var newObj = {};
        for (var i in this) {
            if (this.hasOwnProperty(i)) {
                if (fn(i, this[i], this)) {
                    newObj[i] = this[i];
                }
            }
        }
        return newObj;
    };
}
```

JavaScript objects can become arbitrarily complex trees in modern applications. It
would be nice to be able to find a specific subtree of an object, by a path similar to the
way one might specify a path in a filesystem. This is actually rather easy to accomplish.

The path method takes a path in the form of a Unix file path, */path/to/our/data*. It then uses an inner function to recursively move down the data tree until it finds the requested element and returns it, or realizes the element is not present, in which case it will return undefined. At first glance, it would seem to make sense to just call the top-level path function for each iteration. This would not be a good idea, as it is possible that in some cases there will be an indexed array at some point in the path, causing the iteration to break if the Array.prototype is not the same as the Object.prototype. By doing the search with an inner function, you avoid this problem.

The method in Example 2-24 can handle arrays as well as objects. Both arrays and objects can be addressed with the square bracket notation if a part of the path is a number; for example, [3] will take the fourth element in the array (JavaScript arrays are 0-based).

Example 2-24. Select by path

```
Object.prototype.path = function FindByPath(path) {
    var elementPath = path.split('/');
    var findItter = function findItter(element, path) {
        // If the element is empty just ignore it and move on
        if (path[0] === '') {
            return findItter(element, path.slice(1));
        }
        if (element[path[0]] === undefined) {
            return undefined;
        }
        if (path.length === 1) {
            return element[path[0]];
        }
        return findItter(element[path[0]], path.slice(1));
    };
    return findItter(this, elementPath);
};
```

CHAPTER 3

Testing JavaScript Applications

Test-driven development has become all the rage in software development over the past few years. By creating tests that are automated and repeatable, a developer can have confidence that the code is of high quality and that new changes will not break older features. Some proponents claim that tests should be written before the code they test.

Having a reliable set of tests is a vital part of any software development effort. It enables a developer to have confidence that code works once it's written and will continue to work over time.

Testing has become a key element of development in most server-side development platforms. Solid test harnesses can be found in development environments for PHP, Java, Ruby, and so on. However, the standard method for testing in most of these languages does not work well for JavaScript. Let's look at a few reasons why.

Server-side test suites generally have to test the program under just one set of environments. If a REST service is being built with Python, the tester can build the tests with several safe assumptions. For instance, he may know that it will run on Python version 3.0 on Linux, along with specific versions of all the supporting software.

The web application developer has no such confidence. Users will come to the site using Firefox, Internet Explorer, Chrome, Safari, and Opera—and several versions of each. So test suites must be able to handle testing across a number of browsers and operating systems, each of which is a little bit different.

There are two main sources of differences. First, there are differences in the language itself among the different browsers. For example, the keyword const is supported by Firefox, but not by Internet Explorer. Second, many HTML interfaces exist only in particular browsers or browser versions. For example, many of the various JavaScript interfaces in this book exist only in particular browsers. So tests must be able to adjust to those differences and handle degradation where needed.

Testing experts in Java or C talk about several kinds of tests: unit tests, integration tests, and so on. The base technology of all of these is the same, but the goals of each are different.

Unit tests should be small tests that run fast and test one thing. They should work along the lines that, for a given function/method/interface, if I give it input x it should do y. These test the basic logic of a system. Each unit test should ideally only test one method or very small block of code.

Integration tests are more complex tests that make sure everything is working together correctly. They tend to be more along the lines of "If I click this button, the system should do this."

These ideas don't seem to work as well in JavaScript as they do in other languages. QUnit (see "QUnit" on page 30) seems to be better for unit tests, while Selenium (see "Selenium" on page 33) is better for integration tests. However, the tendency of JavaScript to have lots of small anonymous functions makes running unit tests harder, as those functions can't be easily reached by the testing functions. One aid to testing is to create as many of those functions as possible external to the place they are used, either as part of some larger namespace or as the result of some other function which can be tested.

In Example 3-1, makeInList will return a function that tests whether a field in a record is in a passed list. In this case, the returned function is a pure function with no side effects, so it is easy to test. Example 3-2 shows two tests using a function created by makeInList. If passed "NY," the function returns true because it was created with "NY" in the list, but when passed "CT" it returns false.

Example 3-1. In-list test

```
var makeInList = function (list, field)
{
  return function inList (rec)
  {
      var value = rec[field];
      return list.indexOf(value) !== -1;
  };
};
```

Example 3-2. In-list test used

```
var nynj = makeInList(['NY','NJ'], 'state');
ok(nynj({state: "NY"}));
ok(!nynj({state: "CT"}));
```

Types of Tests

Testers generally talk about several kinds of tests: unit tests, integration tests, and so on. All of these use the same basic tools but work on different levels.

A unit test seeks to test the smallest unit of a code, often a function or method. For instance, Example 3-2 is a unit test. It tests only that function and seeks to check all the possible options for how the code could run.

An integration test is designed to make sure the system as a whole works as designed. An integration test could click a button in the browser and then verify that a record has been updated in a database, which verifies that the whole system is working together. Integration tests often run much slower than unit tests. For this reason, many people run unit tests in real time, but run integration tests overnight.

Acceptance tests verify that the software meets the requirements of the customer. The purpose of these tests is not so much technical—to ensure that it does what the programmer intends—as it is a matter of deployment and meeting user needs.

The runtime model for JavaScript is also more complex. In a server-side language, a unit test generally consists of a few sequential steps:

1. Set up any needed fixtures.
2. Run the method to be tested.
3. Test the results of the method against some criteria.

However, this model does not fit JavaScript, where the results of an action may not be immediate but may happen some time later. A test like this would fail in JavaScript, as there can be a delay between when the method is run and when its results will become available. In JavaScript, testing a test may go more like this:

1. Set up any needed fixtures.
2. Run the method to be tested.
3. Wait for an Ajax call to complete.
4. Check the DOM for the results of the action (including undesired effects on unexpected parts of the page).

An additional complication is that, in many cases, the method to run is a callback on a DOM element. In order to run unit tests in this situation, you really want to find the DOM element and send it the correct event. That way, the handler is invoked in a manner as similar as possible to when an actual user is using the application. Even that is not enough: it doesn't reproduce the experience of a user clicking through various complex interfaces in the DOM.

Browser applications also have the complexity of being based around a user interface. Most test-driven development is done on server interfaces, or data-handling code, where the set of inputs and outputs is relatively constrained. A given function will return one thing when passed input "A" and another when passed input "B."

JavaScript applications are more complicated by centrality of the user interface. The possible range of actions a user can take is by definition very large. So the number of tests needed can be very large and the developer may not even think to create many of them. For example, what happens if a user enters a name with an accent mark into an input field? Will the system react correctly?

QUnit

QUnit is a JavaScript test suite from the same team that produced jQuery. To create a test suite in QUnit, call the test function with two arguments: the test suite name and a function that will actually run the tests.

 It is possible to configure QUnit to complain if any new global variables have been introduced by running a test, and because global variables are one of the major sources of JavaScript bugs, this is a very helpful feature. To test for leaking global variables, add ?noglobals to the URL when starting the tests.

Use of JSLint (see the discussion of JSLint on page 117) can also be very helpful in finding leaking globals and a lot of other errors. It is possible to run JSLint over a set of JavaScript files as part of an automated test suite.

A Simple Example

As an example, let us consider a very trivial Ajax application. In Example 3-3, we have an HTML page with a button. When the button is clicked, the JavaScript handleButtonClick() function will make an Ajax query to the server for a document (in this case, a static HTML document) and then place that document in a <div> in the page. Note that for simplicity I have placed the JavaScript in the document directly. A cleaner implementation would keep the JavaScript in a separate file that the test runner loads along with the tests.

To test this, we want to run the button callback and verify the results are correct. There are two ways that this can be done. The test program could send a click event to the button, or it could call the function directly. For testing in QUnit, it is simpler to call the function directly, but that requires us to bind the function to some variable that can be seen by the test runner. I have done this in the example, assigning the function to the variable handleButtonClick. After calling the callback, the test function waits for a short time to allow the Ajax call to run and then uses jQuery to check if the element is present.

Example 3-3. Simple application

```html
<!DOCTYPE html>
<html>
<head>
  <script src="http://code.jquery.com/jquery-latest.js"></script>
  <script src='button.js'>
  </script>
  <script>
var handleButtonClick = function handleButtonClick(){
  $().get('document.html', '', function(data, status){
        $("<div>").attr({id:'target_div'}).text(data).appendTo('body');
      });
};

$('button.click_me').click(handleButtonClick);
  </script>
  <link rel="stylesheet"
        href="http://github.com/jquery/qunit/raw/master/qunit/qunit.css"
        type="text/css"
        media="screen" />
  <script     src="http://github.com/jquery/qunit/raw/master/qunit/qunit.js"></script>
  <script src='simple-test.js'></script>
</head>

<body>
  <button id='click_me'>Click Me</button>
  <!-- Stuff required by QUnit-->
  <h1 id="qunit-header">QUnit example</h1>
  <h2 id="qunit-banner"></h2>
  <h2 id="qunit-userAgent"></h2>
  <ol id="qunit-tests"></ol>
  <div id="qunit-fixture">test markup, will be hidden</div>
</body>
</html>
```

The QUnit test runner is created by the page on load as any other JavaScript program would be. In this case, it is loaded from *http://github.com/jquery/qunit/raw/master/qunit/qunit.js*. This file will start running any jQuery tests on load. The results of those tests will be shown on the page once the tests are finished running, which is why QUnit requires those elements to be present in the DOM.

To test the example, we'll load QUnit, which the test runner in Example 3-3 does, and then call the handleButtonClick method. Example 3-4 waits for one second for the document to be loaded, by passing a value of 1,000 to the setTimeout method. After that second, it tests whether the <div> exists in the DOM (the first equal call), gets the text from the div, and checks that the first word in the text is "First," which is the expected value (the second equal call). A more complete test may choose to check for that element every quarter-second until it appears or until some maximum time is reached. In the real world, web page load times can vary depending on external factors including network usage and server load.

A test in QUnit is a JavaScript function that is called by the test runner. Look at the simple test in Example 3-4. The test uses several assertion functions that must be satisfied for the test to pass. To test if a value is equal to an expected result, use the equal() method, which takes three methods: the value to test, the expected result, and an optional parameter, which is a message for the test to show if it fails. Using this message will help you to figure out when a test fails. This is even more useful if a test is being looked at six months after it was written.

Example 3-4. Simple test

```
test("Basic Test", function (){
    // assert that the target attribute does not exist
    equal( $('div#target_div').length, 0,
            "Target element should not exist");
    //run method
    handleButtonClick();
    equal( $('div#target_div').length, 0,
            "Target element should still not exist");
    window.setTimeout(function (){
            start();
            equal($('div#target_div').length,1,
                    "Target element should now exist");
            equal("First",
                    $('div#target_div').text().substr(0,5),
                    "Check that the first word is correct");
        }, 1000  );
    stop();
});
```

Testing with QUnit

To run QUnit tests, the qunit stylesheet and JavaScript files must be included in your test runner. These can be pulled directly from GitHub or loaded locally (see Example 3-3). The DOM must also include a few elements that are used by QUnit to display its results. These can be seen in the bottom of the HTML in Example 3-3. That is all that is required to run tests.

QUnit provides eight assertion functions. In addition to equal(), which appeared in our previous example, there are further tests of equality and the ok() method, which tests whether the value passed to it is true. Also, strictEqual() tests according to the JavaScript "===" operator, whereas equal() uses the "==" operator for comparison. To test whether a more complex data structure is the same, use deepEqual(). This does a recursive comparison of the two data structures.

Each equality function has an inverted form that will test for lack of equality: notEqual(), notStrictEqual(), and notDeepEqual(). These take the same parameters as the equal versions but test for the inverted cases.

The final assertion is `raises()`, which takes a function as a parameter and expects it to throw an error conditon.

To test for events that happen in an asynchronous manner, it won't work simply to make a change and return a value. In this case, the test must wait for the action to complete. This can be done by setting a timeout with `setTimeout()`, which will run after a set time. Or it can be done with a callback from some operation, such as an Ajax load or other event.

Selenium

While QUnit lets you test JavaScript code, Selenium (*http://seleniumhq.org/*) takes a different approach. Selenium tests the user interface by simulating the actions that a user may take. A Selenium test will consist of a number of steps that run in a browser, such as loading a page, clicking on a particular element, typing something into a text area, and so on. Interspersed with those actions will be assertions to verify the state of the DOM or other things to be tested. These can include testing that an element or text exists or is absent.

When a Selenium test is run it will actually launch a browser and run it in more or less the same way that the user would. So it is possible to watch the test interacting with the browser. It is even possible to manually interact with the browser while a test is running (though this may not be a great idea).

Selenium consists of several, mostly independent parts. One is an IDE implemented as a browser plug-in for Firefox. Another is the Selenium RC server, *seleniumrc*, a Java server that can be used to automate running tests in different browsers.

The Selenium IDE plug-in for Firefox is a developer's best friend. It allows you to construct tests that are run directly in the browser. The IDE can record the user's actions and replay them as a test later. It also allows you to step through a test one line at a time, which can be very useful for finding timing problems in a test.

 By default, when recording actions, the Selenium IDE will use the IDs of the various HTML elements. When IDs are not explictly assigned by the programmer, some frameworks will assign IDs sequentially as elements are created. These IDs will not be consistent from run to run, so use some other method to identify elements of interest.

The Selenium IDE outputs tests as HTML files that can be run in the IDE itself in Firefox. In addition, these HTML files can be run with the Selenium RC component as a batch job. The Selenium RC server also will allow the HTML tests to be run with any browser, so it is possible to run these tests with IE, Chrome, Opera, or Safari. The Selenium RC server can also be controlled by a traditional test from a test running something like PHPUnit or JUnit.

The Selenium IDE also is useful for recording web macros in development. For example, if you are testing a wizard in your web application that displays four or five screens before the screen that is being debugged, you can use the IDE to create a Selenium script that you can then invoke as a macro to get you automatically to the point being tested.

 If a test works when it is run in single-step mode but not during normal execution, it probably needs a few pause statements to allow the browser to catch up, or even better, some waitFor... statements, which will allow the test and the browser to be in sync.

There are three ways to run tests in Selenium: via the Selenium IDE, from the Selenium RC test runner, and from a programming language. The IDE is easy to use in an interactive setting, but works only with Firefox. The test runner accepts input tests in HTML format, which can be created in the IDE. Finally, it is possible to write tests in a unit test framework in a programming language such as PHPUnit. Using the test runner or the programming language-based test suite allows testing with a full suite of browsers and can provide reporting and other functions. This procedure can also be integrated with continuous integration tools along with any other tests written in any of the xUnit frameworks.

A Selenium test is constructed from an HTML file containing a table, with each step in the test being a row in the table. The row consists of three columns: the command to run, the element on which it will act, and an optional parameter used in some cases. For example, the third column contains the text to type into an input element while testing a form.

Unlike a QUnit test, a Selenium test is all about the user interface. Thus, Selenium is more about integration testing than unit testing. To test Example 3-3 in Selenium, a different approach is required from QUnit. While the QUnit test called the handler function directly, the Selenium test clicks the button and waits for the <div> to show.

This is illustrated in Example 3-5. Each row in the table document performs an action as part of the test. The first row opens the web page to test, then the second line clicks the button (which is identified by the element ID). The test then waits for the page to display the <div>, identified in this case through XPath.

This tests the same simple script as the QUnit test shown in the previous section. However, instead of testing the function itself, it tests the user interface similar to how a human tester may do so. It opens the page and clicks on the click_me button. Then it waits for the target_div to be present in the DOM. It then asserts that the word *First* appears in the page.

Example 3-5. Simple Selenium test

```xml
<?xml version="1.0" encoding="UTF-8"?>
<!DOCTYPE html PUBLIC "-//W3C//DTD XHTML 1.0 Strict//EN"
 "http://www.w3.org/TR/xhtml1/DTD/xhtml1-strict.dtd">
<html xmlns="http://www.w3.org/1999/xhtml" xml:lang="en" lang="en">
<head profile="http://selenium-ide.openqa.org/profiles/test-case">
<meta http-equiv="Content-Type" content="text/html; charset=UTF-8" />
<link rel="selenium.base" href="http://www.example.com/" />
<title>New Test</title>
</head>
<body>
<table cellpadding="1" cellspacing="1" border="1">
<thead>
<tr><td rowspan="1" colspan="3">New Test</td></tr>
</thead><tbody>
<tr>
    <td>open</td>
    <td>/examples/simple.html</td>
    <td></td>
</tr>
<tr>
    <td>click</td>
    <td>click_me</td>
    <td></td>
</tr>
<tr>
    <td>waitForElementPresent</td>
    <td>//div[@id='target_div']</td>
    <td></td>
</tr>
<tr>
    <td>assertTextPresent</td>
    <td>First</td>
    <td></td>
</tr>

<!-- More tests -->
</tbody></table>
</body>
</html>
```

Selenium Commands

Selenium features a rich command language called Selenese (*http://seleniumhq.org/docs/04_selenese_commands.htm*) to allow the programmer to create tests. Pretty much any action that a user could take in the browser can be done in a Selenium command. You can create a Selenium test by creating a script consisting of a series of actions and tests.

Dragging a file from the desktop to the browser (see "Drag-and-Drop" on page 71) is one thing that cannot be done from Selenium, nor can it be easily tested from QUnit.

With very few exceptions, Selenium commands take as a parameter the location of an element in the DOM to be acted on. This location can be specified in one of several ways, including an element ID, an element name, XPath, a CSS class, a JavaScript call into the DOM, and link text. The options are illustrated in "Selenium Location Options" on page 36.

 Using the element ID will not work in ExtJS, as ExtJS assigns IDs to elements that will change each time. Use CSS classes or other properties of the HTML element. To denote buttons, it is often useful to use the text of the button with XPath, like `//button[text()='Save']`. It is also possible to select on an attribute, like `//img[@src='img.png']`.

Selenium Location Options

Selenium offers six ways to address elements on the web page. Using the correct addressing scheme will ease development of tests:

ID
> Supply an HTML ID:
>
> ```
> id
> ```

Name
> Supply an element name (useful for form inputs):
>
> ```
> name=username
> ```

XPath
> Use XPath to find an element:
>
> ```
> //form[@id='loginForm']/input[1]
> ```

CSS
> Find an element by a CSS Selector, a procedure that's familiar to users of jQuery. However, the CSS selector engine in Selenium is more limited than jQuery's:
>
> ```
> css=div.x-btn-text
> ```

Document
> Use the DOM to find an element:
>
> ```
> dom=document.getElementById('loginForm')
> ```

Link text
> Find the text in the `href` attribute (useful for HTML links):
>
> ```
> link='Continue'
> ```

The Selenium base commands do not include any capability for conditionals or loops. A Selenium HTML file is run sequentially from top to bottom, ending when an assertion fails or when the last command is executed. If you need flow control, use the goto_sel_ide.js plug-in (*http://51elliot.blogspot.com/2008/02/selenium-ide-goto.html*).

This plug-in can be useful when looking for memory leaks or other problems that may occur in an application that users will run for a long time. JavaScript still has a way to go to escape from the memory leaks that were not an issue when page reloads were frequent, resetting the state of JavaScript and the DOM.

A large number of commands in Selenium can be used to construct tests. The Selenium IDE contains a reference for commands, so once you have learned some of the basics, you can easily figure out the correct command for any given circumstance. Table 3-1 shows some of the common Selenium commands. They tend to come in two basic groups, *actions* and *assertions*. Actions include such things as click, type, dblclick, keydown, keyup, and many more. Assertions provide the actual tests that allow Selenium to find out how user actions affect the page. Assertions can pause a script but make no changes in the page.

Table 3-1. Selected Selenium commands

Command	Target	Action
open	Web page to open	Opens a web page.
dblclick	Element to double-click	Double-clicks an element.
click	Element to click	Clicks an element.
mouseOver	Element over which to move the mouse	Replicates a mouseOver event.
mouseUp	Element over which to let up the mouse button	Replicates a mouseUp event.
mouseDown	Element on which to press the mouse button down	Replicates a mouseDown event.
type	An XPath selector or other kind of selector to choose the element; the third column is the text to type	Simulates text entry.
windowMaximized		Maximizes the current window.
refresh		Refreshes the browser. Can be useful for resetting JavaScript state.

In ExtJS, or any other custom widget, if a click event does not do what is expected, try using a mouseDown. To select a row in a grid, for example, use a mouseDown event instead of a click. When you click with a mouse, the browser sends three events: mouseDown, mouseUp, and click. Different elements in a user interface may respond to any of them.

Actions in Selenium have two forms: a simple form and a second form that will wait for a page to reload. The waiting form of the `click` command, for instance, is `clickAnd Wait`.

After a sequence of actions, it is necessary to verify that the application actually performed the correct actions. Most tests in Selenium check for the presence or absence of an element or section of text. For example, to test adding a new element to an ExtJS grid, the test script would go something like this:

1. Click the add button.
2. Fill out a form giving default values.
3. Submit a new record to the server.
4. Wait for the server to respond and verify the text is present in the correct grid.

All of the assertions have three fundamental forms: the basic form, a verify form, and a WaitFor form. The basic command will be similar to `assertElementPresent`, and will stop a test when the assertion fails. `verifyElementPresent` will check whether the element exists, but will let the test continue if it does not. This is useful if there are multiple tests and you don't want them to stop after one failure. If an action is supposed to have a result that will be delayed, use `waitForElementPresent`, which will pause the test script until the condition is met or the test times out. In summary:

assert...
> Check that something is true, and stop if it is not.

verify...
> Check that something is true, but continue even if it is false.

waitFor..
> Wait for something to happen on the page (often used with Ajax).

Constructing Tests with the Selenium IDE

Selenium tests can be constructed by hand, but it is often much easier to automate their construction. The Selenium IDE plug-in for Firefox will let you record your actions in the browser and save them as a test. The programmer will still have to put in the assertions and the wait commands manually, and may have to make adjustments to the script that has been produced. The test is saved as an HTML document that can be checked in to version control and run from the IDE as well as from an automatic test runner.

The IDE is a very nice way to try out options in Selenium. It will also let you create test scripts and run them directly from the IDE. The Selenium IDE also allows you to control how fast it executes the scripts, and single-step through them.

The left-side panel (which is hidden in Figure 3-1) shows a list of all the test cases that have been defined. They can all be run with the first button on the toolbar (just to the left of the speed control). The next button to the right executes just one test.

The bottom panel of the Selenium IDE features four tabs (and more can be added with plug-ins). The leftmost tab features a log of tests being run. The second tab is a reference panel. When you select a command from the menu in the middle panel, this tab will show information about the selected command, including what arguments it takes.

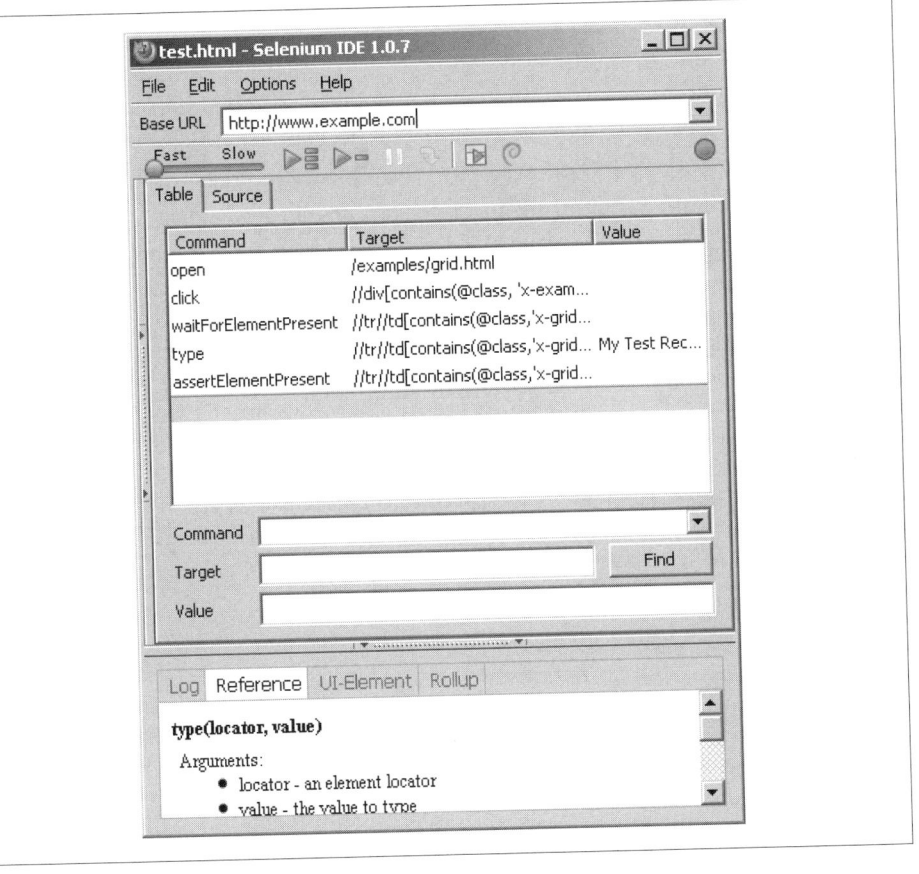

Figure 3-1. Selenium IDE

Automatically Running Tests

It is possible to use one of the popular test suites (such as JUnit or PHPUnit) to run Selenium tests, letting the tests run across multiple browsers and platforms. If you are running a regular set of unit tests, Selenium tests can be run from your normal test runner (see Example 3-6).

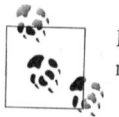 Most or all of what is described here for PHPUnit should also work with minor modifications in all similar test suites for other languages.

These tests will run just like any other test in the test enviroment. Each HTML file will run as a test in the test suite. (Details of this may vary depending on which test runner is being used.) The test runner will run each HTML file in sequence in a manner similar to what was done in the IDE.

To run tests from PHPUnit, one or more test machines need to be designated to run the browsers. Each test machine needs a copy of the Selenium RC program running and must have the browser or browsers being tested installed on the machine. The *seleniumrc* binary is a Java *.jar* file, so it will run on Windows, Linux, or the Mac.

When a test is run in PHPUnit, the test class `PHPUnit_Extensions_SeleniumTestCase` will contact the *seleniumrc* program and ask it to start up a browser instance and then send it commands over a REST interface.

If multiple browsers are listed in the `$browsers` static member, or via a *phpunit.xml* file (see Example 3-7), the `PHPUnit_Extensions_SeleniumTestCase` class will run each test for each browser in sequence. In Example 3-6, for instance, it will run the tests on Safari, Firefox, Chrome, and Internet Explorer. Often it is better to list the browser options in the *phpunit.xml* file, because you can then create multiple files to help you change test options without changing test source code.

The following test just runs one Selenium test from the file *seleneseTest.html*. However, we could have it automatically run an entire directory of Selenium HTML test files by setting the `$seleneseDirectory` property of the test class to the path to the files:

```
public static $seleneseDirectory = '/path/to/files';
```

Example 3-6. Running Selenium from PHPUnit

```php
<?php
require_once 'PHPUnit/Extensions/SeleniumTestCase.php';

class WebTest extends PHPUnit_Extensions_SeleniumTestCase
{
    protected $captureScreenshotOnFailure = TRUE;
    protected $screenshotPath = '/var/www/localhost/htdocs/screenshots';
    protected $screenshotUrl = 'http://localhost/screenshots';

    public static $browsers = array(
      array(
        'name'    => 'Safari on MacOS X',
        'browser' => '*safari',
        'host'    => 'mac.testbox',
        'port'    => 4444,
        'timeout' => 30000
      ),
```

```php
    array(
        'name'    => 'Firefox on Windows',
        'browser' => '*firefox',
        'host'    => 'windows.testbox',
        'port'    => 4444,
        'timeout' => 30000
    ),
    array(
        'name'    => 'Chrome on Windows XP',
        'browser' => '*googlechrome',
        'host'    => 'windows.testbox',
        'port'    => 4444,
        'timeout' => 30000
    ),
    array(
        'name'    => 'Internet Explorer on Windows XP',
        'browser' => '*iexplore',
        'host'    => 'windows.testbox',
        'port'    => 4444,
        'timeout' => 30000
    )
);

    protected function setUp()
    {
        $this->setBrowserUrl('http://www.example.com/');
    }

    public function testSeleniumFile()
    {
        $this->open('http://www.example.com/');
        $this->runSelenese('seleneseTest.html');
    }

}
?>
```

Example 3-7. phpunit.xml

```xml
<phpunit stopOnFailure="true"
    verbose="true"
    strict="true">
  <php>

  </php>
  <selenium>
    <browser name="Firefox"
        browser="*firefox"
        host="192.168.0.10"
        port="4444"
        timeout="30000"/>
    <browser name="Chrome"
        browser="*chrome"
        host="192.168.0.10"
        port="4444"
        timeout="30000"/>
```

```
      <!-- Other Browsers -->
    </selenium>
    <testsuites>
      <testsuite name="Selenium">
        <file>/path/to/MyTest.php</file>
      </testsuite>
    </testsuites>

</phpunit>
```

With all the advantages of Selenium RC, it has one major drawback: it can run only one test at a time. So if you have a large test suite and a number of different browsers to run that test suite, the full test run can take many hours. Selenium Grid provides a solution to this, letting you run a number of tests in parallel on a group of machines. The Selenium Grid software along with examples and documentation can be found at *http://selenium-grid.seleniumhq.org/*.

If you don't want to build your own test farm, there are cloud Selenium farms on the Web that you can use. In addition, it is possible to run Selenium on Amazon's EC2 cloud service. This can be very useful for occasional users or for a new startup that may not have the resources to build and maintain a local Selenium farm. This can also be very helpful in seeing how an application will perform over a remote network.

Selenese Command Programming Interface

The Selenium test suite can run a test from an HTML file or directly from the unit test code. The Selenium RC server also has an API that can be called from unit test code in several languages. You can write tests for Selenium in PHP, Ruby, Python, Java, C#/.NET, and Perl. You can create code test cases for all of these languages via the Selenium IDE or by hand. The Selenium IDE will generate the skeleton of a test for you. To do this, record a test in the IDE, choose the output option for the language in which to run the test. The tests will be converted to that language.

> To run Selenium on several browsers, you need to set up the Selenium server. See "Selenium RC and a Test Farm" on page 46.

Running Selenium directly from a unit test gives you the full power of the host language, notably its flow control, while the HTML-style tests are much more limited. By using the API from a server-side programming language, it is possible to create a very rich environment for scripting the Web, and of course you have access to libraries on the server side to check data in a database or access web services. You can construct a test that will perform some actions in the browser, and then check the result in a database or against a logfile.

Another advantage of server-side testing is that if you are using any form of continuous integration, such as CruiseControl or phpUnderControl, the Selenium tests appear to the test system as just more tests in whatever language the team is using. In a team that is using a test framework, this will leverage the existing experience of the team.

Example 3-8 is a very simple Selenium test, written in PHP with the PHPUnit testing framework. It just opens up a web page, and after the page has loaded, it asserts that the title of the page is the string "Hello World." It will then click a button with the text "Click Me." If the title is not "Hello World" or there is no such button, the test will fail.

Example 3-8. Testing Hello World

```php
<?php
require_once 'PHPUnit/Extensions/SeleniumTestCase.php';

class WebTest extends PHPUnit_Extensions_SeleniumTestCase
{
  function testTitle()
  {
    $this->open('http://www.example.com/');
    $this->assertTitle('Hello World');
    $this->click("//button[text()='Click Me']");
  }
}
```

In general, Selenese commands consist of actions, assertions, and queries. The actions reflect the basic forms of Selenium actions: click, mouseOver, mouseDown, type, and so on. The various delayed forms that appear in the Selenium IDE are not present, but can be easily simulated by using a loop with a sleep function.

Many of the useful utility methods that are present in the HTML Selenium test runner are not present in the server-side Selenese interface. Methods such as WaitForElement Present (see Example 3-9) or WaitForElementNotPresent are not included, but can be easily added by creating a custom base class for the tests and adding them there.

Example 3-9. WaitForElementPresent

```php
function waitForElementPresent($el, $timeout = 60)
{
  while($timeout)
  {
    if($this->isElementPresent($el))
    {
      return true;
    }
    $timeout -= 1;
    sleep(1);
  }
  $this->fail("Element $el not found");
}
```

Queries allow the programmer to determine the state of the page after actions have happened. These queries allow the programmer to find out whether an element or piece of text exists on the page, or otherwise find out about the current state of the page.

The Selenese API also features a number of methods to get data from the HTML document in the context of a unit test. To test whether a given text is present in the page, use the method $this->isTextPresent(), which is often quite useful to find out if an element is present or absent. To find out whether an element exists, use the method $this->isElementPresent(). To actually retrieve text from the DOM, use the $this->getText() method. This will take any form of selector that Selenium can accept and will return the text of that element. If the element is not present, the method will throw an exception.

The XPath selector matches multiple elements on the page. It will normally return the first matched element. To find out how many elements are matched, use $this->getX pathCount().

When building tests in PHP, synchronizing the test actions between the interface in the browser and the test running in PHP can be a challenge. It is intuitive to write a test that does something such as click one element and then immediately mouse over another. This will inevitably fail, as the JavaScript will take some time (maybe 0.1 second) to create a piece of the user interface or wait for data to load from the server. There are two ways to handle this.

The simple way is to place delays in the PHP code. A few well-placed sleep() commands can cause a test to function correctly. However, this may cause a test to take longer to run than is necessary. To speed up tests, something like a waitForElementPresent() call with a 1/10 of a second delay between testing can cause the script to run faster, as long as there is a way to tell from the DOM when the browser is ready for the next step in the test.

The second way is to use the $this->getEval() method in the Selenese interface to evaluate custom JavaScript. Pass this method a string that contains the JavaScript to be executed. When you call JavaScript via getEval(), it will run in the window context of the test runner window, not the test window. Therefore, global variables must be prefixed by the global window object, which normally is not required.

In Example 3-10, Selenium executes getEval() in JavaScript in order to extract the global session_id variable.

Example 3-10. Running JavaScript from Selenese

```
$session_id = $this->getEval('window.session_id'):
```

It is also possible to use Selenium RC to set up manual tests, by having the script open the page and perform all the steps leading up to the point where you need to test things. When it gets to the end point, it should pause for an extended period of time because the browser will close when the test ends. At the point that the test stops, a human can take over the browser and perform any manual actions that might be needed. This is often helpful when developing a multistep wizard or similar user interface.

Running QUnit from Selenium

Selenium can run QUnit tests as well. To do so, load the QUnit page in Selenium and run the tests. It is also possible to choose to only run a subset of tests by passing parameters to the URL string. By integrating Selenium with QUnit, you can export the results of browser tests in QUnit into a test runner for continuous integration.

Selenium just opens the QUnit URL and then stands back and waits for the test to finish. To let the test runner know whether the tests passed or failed, QUnit provides a simple micro format (see Example 3-12) that shows how many tests were run and how many passed or failed. The unit test can then look for this data by an XPath selector and make sure all tests passed.

In Example 3-11, the PHP program opens the QUnit test from the start of this chapter and then waits for the test to run. When the test finishes, the `qunit-testresult` element will be inserted into the DOM. At this point Selenium can find the number of tests that were run and how many passed or failed. Example 3-13 shows the PHP code to extract the results of QUnit tests from Selenium.

Example 3-11. Selenium test to run QUnit

```php
<?php
require_once 'PHPUnit/Extensions/SeleniumTestCase.php';

class WebTest extends PHPUnit_Extensions_SeleniumTestCase
{
  function testQUnit()
  {
    //Put the URL of your HTML file with the QUnit test here
    $this->open('http://host.com/simple.html');

    $this->waitForElementPresent("//p[@id='qunit-testresult']");
    $failCount  = $this->getText("//p[@id='qunit-testresult']/span[@class='failed']");
    $passCount  = $this->getText("//p[@id='qunit-testresult']/span[@class='passed']");
    $totalCount = $this->getText("//p[@id='qunit-testresult']/span[@class='total']");
    $this->assertEquals($passCount, $totalCount,
                "Check that all tests passed $passCount of $totalCount passed");
    $this->assertEquals("0", $failCount,
                "Checking result of QUnit tests $failCount/$totalCount tests failed");

  }
```

```
function waitForElementPresent($element, $timeout = 60)
{
  $time = 0;
  while(!$this->isElementPresent($element))
    {
      $time++;
      if($time > $timeout)
      {
          throw New Exception("Timeout: $element not found!");
      }
      sleep(1);
    }
  }
}
```

Example 3-12. QUnit result micro format

```
<p id="qunit-testresult" class="result">
  Tests completed in 221 milliseconds.<br/>
  <span class="passed">1</span> tests of
  <span class="total">2</span> passed,
  <span class="failed">1</span> failed.
</p>
```

Example 3-13. PHP code to extract data from QUnit

```
<?php
$failCount  = $this->getText("//p[@id='qunit-testresult']/span[@class='failed']");
$passCount  = $this->getText("//p[@id='qunit-testresult']/span[@class='passed']");
$totalCount = $this->getText("//p[@id='qunit-testresult']/span[@class='total']");
$this->assertEquals($passCount, $totalCount,
                    "Check that all tests passed $passCount of $totalCount passed");
$this->assertEquals("0", $failCount,
                    "Checking result of QUnit tests $failCount/$totalCount tests failed");
```

Selenium RC and a Test Farm

It is important to make sure an application runs well not just on one browser, but on a large number of browsers and platforms. In most cases you can assume that your application may be run on Windows XP, Windows Vista, Windows 7, Mac OS X, and Linux. In addition, users may be using some combination of Firefox, Chrome, Internet Explorer, Safari, and Opera, and probably several different versions of each.

The implementations of JavaScript and various interfaces are similar among these different browsers, and using a framework like jQuery will smooth over some of the differences, but the browsers are still not exactly the same. So code that works well in Firefox may suddenly break in Chrome or Safari. And, of course, code could work well in one version of a browser but not on an older or newer version. So testing across a wide matrix of browsers is vital. However, it is probably too much to expect a QA team to do this manually, hence the need for automation.

Selenium RC makes it possible to test all of these various combinations using a network of machines. Each test machine must have Java installed. In many cases, Java will be installed by default, but if it is not, download and install it. Then download and unpack the Selenium RC package from *http://seleniumhq.org/download/*. On each server, start the Selenium server JAR with the command that follows. It is probably a good idea to have the Selenium server start up automatically on machine boot in the case of a machine that will be a member of a test farm. Normally the Selenium server will be installed with reasonable defaults, but it offers a number of command-line options that allow some degree of customization. Specifically, you can change the port from the default 4444, if needed, with the -**port** option. This can be used to run several instances of the server on one server in order to test on several browsers at once:

```
java -jar selenium-server.jar [-port 4444]
```

It is not necessary to use a separate physical machine for each test server. Any of the common virtual machine technologies can work well for this. A reasonably powerful server with enough RAM should be able to run a small but useful virtual test farm.

If you need to test your application on Android or iOS Selenium, you can do that as well. There is an Android driver (*http://code.google.com/p/selenium/wiki/Android Driver*) for Selenium, as well as an iPhone driver (*http://code.google.com/p/selenium/wiki/IPhoneDriver*). Note that in order to run the iPhone driver you need to have a Mac as well as the iPhone development setup. Because the Selenium driver is not in the iPhone store, you need to be able to install it on your phone with a provisioning profile, or use the simulator in Xcode.

CHAPTER 4

Local Storage

The web browser provides JavaScript users a wonderful environment for building applications that run in the browser. Using ExtJS or jQuery, it is possible to build an app that for many users can rival what can be done in a desktop application, and provide a method of distribution that is about as simple as it gets. But however nice the browser has been in terms of providing a user experience, it has fallen flat when it comes to data storage.

Historically, browsers did not have any way to store data. They were, in effect, the ultimate thin client. The closest that could happen was the HTTP cookie mechanism, which allows a piece of data to be attached to each HTTP request. However, cookies suffer from several problems. First, each cookie is sent back and forth with every request. So the browser sends the cookie for each JavaScript file, image, Ajax request, and so on. This can add a lot of bandwidth use for no good reason. Second, the cookie specification tried to make it so that a cookie could be shared among different subdomains. If a company had `app.test.com` and `images.test.com`, a cookie could be set to be visible to both. The problem with this is that outside of the United States, three-part domain names become common. For example, it would be possible to set a cookie for all the hosts in `.co.il` that would allow a cookie to leak to almost every host in Israel. And it is not possible to simply require a three-part domain name whenever the name contains a country suffix, because some countries such as Canada do not follow the same convention.

Having local storage on the browser can be a major advantage in terms of speed. A normal Ajax query can take anywhere from half a second to several seconds to execute, depending on the server. However, even in the best possible case it can be quite slow. A simple ICMP ping between my office in Tel Aviv and a server in California will take an average of about 250 ms. Of that 250 ms, a large part is probably due to basic physical limitations: data can travel down the wire at just some fraction of the speed of light. So there is very little that can be done to make that go faster, as long as the data has to travel between browser and server.

Local storage options are a very good option for data that is static or mostly static. For example, many applications have a list of countries as part of their data. Even if the list includes some extra information, such as whether a product is being offered in each country, the list will not change very often. In this case, it often works to have the data preloaded into a localStorage object, and then do a conditional reload when necessary so that the user will get any fresh data, but not have to wait for the current data.

Local storage is, of course, also essential for working with a web application that may be offline. Although Internet access may seem to be everywhere these days, it should not be regarded as universal, even on smartphones. Users with devices such as the iPod touch will have access to the Internet only where there is WiFi, and even smartphones like the iPhone or Android will have dead zones where there is no access.

With the development of HTML5, a serious movement has grown to provide the browser with a way to create persistent local storage, but the results of this movement have yet to gel. There are currently at least three different proposals for how to store data on the client.

In 2007, as part of Gears, Google introduced a browser-based SQLite database. WebKit-based browsers, including Chrome, Safari, and the browsers on the iPhone and Android phones, have implemented a version of the Gears SQLite database. However, SQLite was dropped from the HTML5 proposal because it is a single-sourced component.

The localStorage mechanism provides a JavaScript object that persists across web reloads. This mechanism seems to be reasonably well agreed on and stable. It is good for storing small-sized data such as session information or user preferences.

This current chapter explains how to use current localStorage implementations. In Chapter 5, we'll look at a more complicated and sophisticated form of local storage that has appeared on some browsers: IndexedDB.

The localStorage and sessionStorage Objects

Modern browsers provide two objects to the programmer for storage, localStorage and sessionStorage. Each can hold data as keys and values. They have the same interface and work in the same way, with one exception. The localStorage object is persistent across browser restarts, while the sessionStorage object resets itself when a browser session restarts. This can be when the browser closes or a window closes. Exactly when this happens will depend on the specifics of the browser.

Setting and getting these objects is pretty simple, as shown in Example 4-1.

Example 4-1. Accessing localStorage

```
//set
localStorage.sessionID = sessionId;
localStorage.setItem('sessionID', sessionId);
```

```
//get

var sessionId;
sessionId = localStorage.sessionID;
sessionId = localStorage.getItem('sessionId');

localStorage.sessionId = undefined;
localStorage.removeItem('sessionId');
```

Browser storage, like cookies, implements a "same origin" policy, so different websites can't interfere with one another or read one another's data. But both of the storage objects in this section are stored on the user's disk (as cookies are), so a sophisticated user can find a way to edit the data. Chrome's Developer Tools allow a programmer to edit the storage object, and you can edit it in Firefox via Firebug or some other tool. So, while other sites can't sneak data into the storage objects, these objects still should not be trusted.

Cookies are burdened with certain restrictions: they are limited to about 4 KB in size and must be transmitted to the server with every Ajax request, greatly increasing network traffic. The browser's localStorage is much more generous. The HTML5 specification does not list an exact size limit for its size, but most browsers seem to limit it to about 5 MB per web host. The programmer should not assume a very large storage area.

Data can be stored in a storage object with direct object access or with a set of access functions. The session object can store only strings, so any object stored will be typecast to a string. This means an object will be stored as [object Object], which is probably not what you want. To store an object or array, convert it to JSON first.

Whenever a value in a storage object is changed, it fires a storage event. This event will show the key, its old value, and its new value. A typical data structure is shown in Example 4-2. Unlike some events, such as clicks, storage events cannot be prevented. There is no way for the application to tell the browser to not make a change. The event simply informs the application of the change after the fact.

Example 4-2. Storage event interface

```
var storageEvent = {
    key: 'key',
    oldValue: 'old',
    newValue: 'newValue',
    url: 'url',
    storageArea: storage // the storage area that changed
};
```

WebKit provides a screen in its Developer Tools where a programmer can view and edit the localStorage and sessionStorage objects (see Figure 4-1). From the Developer Tools, click on the Storage tab. This will show the localStorage and sessionStorage objects for a page. The Storage screen is also fully editable: keys can be added, deleted, and edited there.

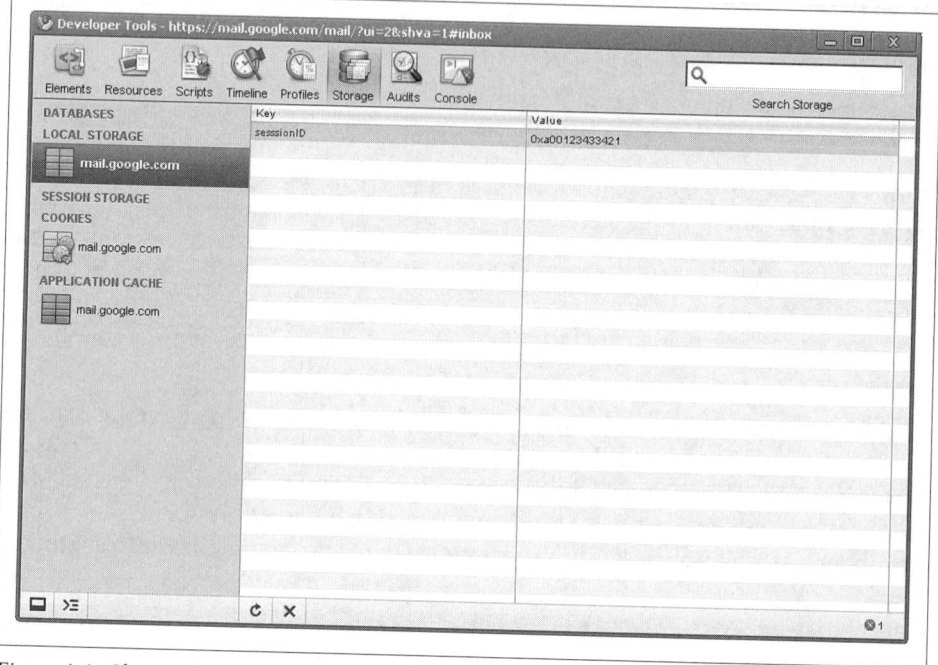

Figure 4-1. Chrome Storage Viewer

Although Firebug does not provide an interface to the `localStorage` and `sessionStor age` objects as Chrome and other WebKit-based browsers do, the objects can be accessed via the JavaScript console, and you can add, edit, and delete keys there. Given time, I expect someone will write a Firebug extension to do this.

Of course, it is possible to write a customized interface to view and edit the storage objects on any browser. Create a widget on-screen that exposes the objects using the `getItem` and `removeItem` calls shown in Example 4-1 and allow editing through text boxes. The skeleton of a widget is shown in Example 4-3.

Example 4-3. Storage Viewer

```
(function createLocalStorageViewer()
{
  $('<table></table>').attr(
  {
    "id": "LocalStorageViewer",
    "class": 'hidden viewer'
  }).appendTo('body');

  localStorage.on('update', viewer.load);
```

```
var viewer =
{
  load: function loadData()
  {
    var data, buffer;
    var renderLine = function (line)
    {
      return "<tr key='{key}' value='{value}'>\n".populate(line) +
        "<td class='remove'>Remove Key</td>" +
        "<td class='storage-key'>{key}</td><td>{value}</td></tr>".populate(line);
    };

    buffer = Object.keys(localStorage).map(function (key)
    var rec =
    {
      key: key,
      value: localStorage[data]
    };
    return rec;
    });

  };

  $("#LocalStorageViewer").html(buffer.map(renderLine).join(''));

  $("#LocalStorageViewer tr.remove").click(function ()
  {
    var key = $(this).parent('tr').attr('key').remove();
    localStorage[key] = undefined;
  });

  $("#LocalStroageViewer tr").dblclick(function ()
  {
    var key = $(this).attr('key');
    var value = $(this).attr('value');
    var newValue = prompt("Change Value of " + key + "?", value);
    if (newValue !== null)
    {
      localStorage[key] = newValue;
    }
  });
};
}());
```

Using localStorage in ExtJS

ExtJS, some examples of which appeared in earlier chapters, is a very popular JavaScript framework allowing very sophisticated interactive displays. This section shows how to use localStorage with ExtJS.

One nice feature of ExtJS is that many of its objects can remember their state. For example, the ExtJS grid object allows the user to resize, hide and show, and reorder columns, and these changes are remembered and redisplayed when a user comes back to the application later. This allows each user to customize the way the elements of an application work.

ExtJS provides an object to save state, but uses cookies to store the data. A complex application can create enough state to exceed the size limits of cookies. An application with a few dozen grids can overflow the size of a cookie, which can lock up the application. So it would be much nicer to use `localStorage`, taking advantage of its much larger size and avoiding the overhead of sending the data to the server on every request.

Setting up a custom state provider object is, in fact, pretty easy. The provider shown in Example 4-4 extends the generic provider object and must provide three methods: `set`, `clear`, and `get`. These methods simply read and write the data into the store. In Example 4-4, I have chosen to index the data in the store with the rather simple method of using the string `state_` with the state ID of the element being saved. This is a reasonable method.

Example 4-4. ExtJS local state provider

```
Ext.ux.LocalProvider = function() {
    Ext.ux.LocalProvider.superclass.constructor.call(this);
};

Ext.extend(Ext.ux.LocalProvider, Ext.state.Provider, {
    //************************************************************
    set: function(name, value) {
        if (typeof value == "undefined" || value === null) {
            localStorage['state_' + name] = undefined;
            return;
        }
        else {
            localStorage['state_' + name] = this.encodeValue(value);
        }
    },

    //************************************************************
    // private
    clear: function(name) {
        localStorage['state_' + name] = undefined;
    },

    //************************************************************
    get: function(name, defaultValue) {
        return Ext.value(this.decodeValue(localStorage['state_' + name]), defaultValue);
    }
});

// set up the state handler
Ext.onReady(function setupState() {
    var provider = new Ext.ux.LocalProvider();
    Ext.state.Manager.setProvider(provider);
});
```

It would also be possible to have all the state data in one large object and to store it into one key in the store. This has the advantage of not creating a large number of elements in the store, but makes the code more complex. In addition, if two windows try to update the store, one could clobber the changes made by the other. The local storage solution in this chapter offers no great solution to the issue of race conditions. In places where it can be a problem, it is probably better to use IndexedDB or some other solution.

Offline Loading with a Data Store

When some of the persistent data used in an application will be relatively static, it can make sense to load it to local storage for faster access. In this case, the Ext.data.Json Store object will need to be modified so that its load() method will look for the data in the localStorage area before attempting to load the data from the server. After loading the data from localStorage, Ext.data.JsonStore should call the server to check whether the data has changed. By doing this, the application can make the data available to the user right away at the cost of possibly short-term inconsistency. This can make a user interface feel faster to the user and reduce the amount of bandwidth that the application uses.

For most requests, the data will not have changed, so using some form of ETag for the data makes a great deal of sense. The data is requested from the server with an HTTP GET request and an If-None-Match header. If the server determines that the data has not changed, it can send back a 304 Not Modified response. If the data has changed, the server sends back the new data, and the application loads it into both the Ext.data.Json Store object and the sessionStorage object.

The Ext.data.PreloadStore object (see Example 4-6) stores data into the session cache as one large JSON object (see Example 4-5). It further wraps the data that the server sends back in a JSON envelope, which allows it to store some metadata with it. In this case, the ETag data is stored as well as the date when the data is loaded.

Example 4-5. Ext.data.PreloadStore offline data format

```
{
    "etag": "25f9e794323b453885f5181f1b624d0b",
    "loadDate": "26-jan-2011",
    "data": {
        "root": [{
            "code": "us",
            "name": "United States"
        },
        {
            "code": "ca",
            "name": "Canada"
        }]
    }
}
```

 When building an ETag, make sure to use a good hash function. MD5 is probably the best choice. SHA1 can also be used, but since it produces a much longer string it is probably not worthwhile. In theory, it is possible to get an MD5 collision, but in practice it is probably not something to worry about for cache control.

Data in the `localStorage` object can be changed in the background. As I already explained, the user can change the data from the Chrome Developer Tools or from the Firebug command line. Or it can just happen unexpectedly because the user has two browsers open to the same application. So it is important for the store to listen for an update event from the `localStorage` object.

Most of the work is done in the `beforeload` event handler. This handler checks the data store for a cached copy of the data, and if it is there, it loads it into the store. If there is data present, the handler will reload the data as well, but will use the `Function.defer()` method to delay the load until a time when the system has hopefully finished loading the web page so that doing the load will be less likely to interfere with the user.

The `store.doConditionalLoad()` method makes an Ajax call to the server to load the data. It includes the `If-None-Match` header so that, if the data has not changed, it will load the current data. It also includes a `force` option that will cause the `beforeload` handler to actually load new data and not try to refresh the store from the `localStorage` cached version of the object.

I generally define constants for `SECOND`, `MINUTE`, and `HOUR` simply to make the code more readable.

Example 4-6. Ext.data.PreloadStore

```
Ext.extend(Ext.data.PreloadStore, Exta.data.JsonStore, {
  indexKey: '',

  //default index key
  loadDefer: Time.MINUTE,
  // how long to defer loading the data
  listeners: {
    load: function load(store, records, options)
    {
      var etag = this.reader.etag;
      var jsonData = this.reader.jsonData;
      var data =
      {
        etag: etag,
        date: new date(),
        data: jsonData
      };
      sessionStorage[store.indexKey] = Ext.encode(data);

    },
```

```
beforeload: function beforeLoad(store, options)
{
    var data = sessionStorage[store.indexKey];
    if (data === undefined || options.force)
    {
        return true; // Cache miss, load from server
    }
    var raw = Ext.decode(data);
    store.loadData(raw.data);
    // Defer reloading the data until later
    store.doConditionalLoad.defer(store.loadDefer, store, [raw.etag]);
    return false;
}
},
doConditionalLoad: function doConditionalLoad(etag)
{

    this.proxy.headers["If-None-Match"] = etag;
    this.load(
    {
        force: true
    });

},
forceLoad: function ()
{
    // Pass in a bogus ETag to force a load
    this.doConditionalLoad('');
}
});
```

Storing Changes for a Later Server Sync

In the event that an application may be used offline, or with a flaky connection to the
Internet, it can be nice to provide the user a way to save her changes without actually
needing the network to be present. To do this, write the changes in each record to a
queue in the localStorage object. When the browser is online again, the queue can be
pushed to the server. This is similar in intent to a transaction log as used in a database.

A save queue could look like Example 4-7. Each record in the queue represents an
action to take on the server. The exact format will of course be determined by the needs
of a specific application.

Example 4-7. Save queue data

```
[
    {
        "url": "/index.php",
        "params": {}
    },
    {
        "url": "/index.php",
        "params": {}
```

```
        },
        {
            "url": "/index.php",
            "params": {}
        }
    ]
```

Once the web browser is back online, it will be necessary to process the items in the queue. Example 4-8 takes the queue and sends the first element to the server. If that request is a success, it will take the next element and continue walking down the queue until the entire queue has been sent. Even if the queue is long, this process will execute it with minimal effect on the user because Ajax processes each item in an asynchronous manner. To reduce the number of Ajax calls, it would also be possible to change this code to send the queue items in groups of, say, five at a time.

Example 4-8. Save queue

```
var save = function save(queue)
{
  if (queue.length > 0)
  {
    $.ajax(
    {
      url: 'save.php',
      data: queue.slice(0, 5),
      success: function (data, status, request)
      {
        save(queue.slice(5));
      }
    });
  }
};
```

JQuery Plug-ins

If the uncertainty of all the client-side storage options is enough to drive you crazy, you have other options. As with many things in JavaScript, a bad and inconsistent interface can be covered up with a module that provides a much better interface. Here are two such modules that can make life easier.

DSt

DSt (*http://github.com/gamache/DSt*) is a simple library that wraps the `localStorage` object. DSt can be a freestanding library or work as a jQuery plug-in. It will automatically convert any complex object to a JSON structure.

DSt can also save and restore the state of a form element or an entire form. To save and restore an element, pass the element or its ID to the `DSt.store()` method. To restore it later, pass the element to the `DSt.recall()` method.

To store the state of an entire form, use the `DSt.store_form()` method. It takes the ID or element of the form itself. The data can be restored with the `DSt.populate_form()` method. Example 4-9 shows the basic use of DSt.

Example 4-9. DSt interface

```
$.DSt.set('key', 'value');
var value = $.DSt.get('key');

$.DSt.store('element'); // Store the value of a form element
$.DSt.recall('element'); // Recall the value of a form element

$.DSt.store_form('form');
$.DSt.populate_form('form');
```

jStore

If you don't want to venture to figure out which storage engines are supported on which browsers and create different code for each case, there is a good solution: the jStore (*http://twablet.com/docs.html?p=jstore*) plug-in for jQuery. This supports `localStorage`, `sessionStorage`, Gears SQLite, and HTML5 SQLite, as well as Flash Storage and IE 7's proprietary solution.

The jStore plug-in has a simple interface that allows the programmer to store name/value pairs in any of its various storage engines. It provides one set of interfaces for all the engines, so the program can degrade gracefully when needed in situations where a storage engine doesn't exist on a given browser.

The jStore plug-in provides a list of engines that are available in the `jQuery.jStore.Availability` instance variable. The program should select the engine that makes the most sense. For applications that require multibrowser support, this can be a useful addition. See the jStore web page for more details.

CHAPTER 5

IndexedDB

The `localStorage` interface (see Chapter 4) provides a very nice interface for storing small amounts of data, but the browser limits this storage space to 5 MB in many cases. If the storage needs of an application go beyond that, or if the application needs to have query access to structured data, local storage is not the best choice. In this case, having a more robust storage mechanism can be useful for the application developer. IndexedDB provides this mechanism on many browsers. For example, a programmer may store product catalog data into an IndexedDB store so that when the user searches for an item, the server does not need to make a trip to the server to find the data for a particular item.

IndexedDB is a NoSQL database that will feel familiar to people who have used such products as MongoDB or CouchDB. A program can store JavaScript objects directly into an IndexedDB data store.

IndexedDB has been in Firefox starting with version 4. It also was introduced into Google Chrome starting with version 11. Microsoft has a version online at its HTML5 Labs website (*http://html5labs.interoperabilitybridges.com/*) as an ActiveX control, which can be added into IE, and presumably it will be in the main IE release at some point. It will probably be available in other browsers in the next year or two. Formally, IndexedDB is now a draft proposal from the W3C (*http://dvcs.w3.org/hg/IndexedDB/raw-file/tip/Overview.html*).

 Because IndexedDB is supported by only two browsers at this point, use should probably be restricted to internal applications where you can limit use to browsers of your choice. Using it in a general app should be done with extreme caution, as Microsoft Internet Explorer, Opera, and Safari do not support this feature yet (at least as of November 2011).

Like `localStorage`, IndexedDB has a strict same-origin policy. So a database created by one page cannot be accessed by pages on other hosts. This provides a level of security for data, in that it is protected from scripts running on other pages. But any script running on the page that created the database has full access to the database, and of course the user has access to the data.

IndexedDB has several advantages over SQLite. First, its native data storage format is a JavaScript object. There is no need to map a JavaScript object into a SQL table structure, which is always a poor fit and can allow for SQL injection attacks. Injection attacks can't happen with IndexedDB, though in some cases XSS could be a problem, if a user manages to inject JavaScript into the store and have it put back into a page.

The IndexedDB data store provides a set of interfaces to store JavaScript objects on a local disk. Each object must have a key by which objects can be retrieved, and may also have secondary keys.

Like many native JavaScript interfaces, IndexedDB turns out to be very verbose and a bit of a pain to use. However, also like many other JavaScript interfaces, it has been wrapped into a very nice API in the form of a jQuery plug-in. This chapter will show all examples using that plug-in because the code is much easier to understand than the raw IndexedDB interface, and this is how I would recommend using IndexedDB if you have a choice in the matter.

I will show a number of examples around a theoretical book search application. Each line of data will be formatted like Example 5-1. We will also create indexes on various fields to show how they are used.

Example 5-1. Example data record

```
{
    "title": "Real World Haskell",
    "price": 49.95,
    "price_can": 49.95,
    "authors": [
        "Bryan O'Sullivan",
        "John Goerzen",
        "Don Stewart"
    ],
    "cover_animal": "Rhinocerus Beetle",
    "cover_url": "http://....",
    "topics": ["Haskell"]
}
```

IndexedDB keeps applications and related data stores in sync as they evolve, through a built-in version system. Each data store has a version that an application can check when it loads. If the version is not current, the application can then take appropriate actions to make it current by creating new object stores and indexes. The jQuery IndexedDB interface will increment the version as needed when changes to the structure happen, so this is now handled automatically.

Versions should be changed when a new data store is being added, or an index is being added. When an index or store is removed, a version must also be changed. The jQuery IndexedDB module will do this automatically. Simply having an application check that the various `objectStores` and indexes exist will ensure that the schema is correct. If an index does not exist as in Example 5-2 it will be created automatically.

Example 5-2. Creating an index

```
$.indexeddb(db).objectStore(objectStore).index(field);
```

Interactions with IndexedDB must be done by way of transactions. This is because the IndexedDB interface is asynchronous, and IndexedDB can be accessed from a Web Worker or a second window running another thread (each window in JavaScript runs its own thread). So, even though simultaneous accesses will be rare, it is possible for more than one JavaScript thread to access a given IndexedDB database at the same time, and the interface must protect against race conditions.

> The IndexedDB interface spec includes a synchronous version of the interface that can be used in Web Workers, but it has not been implemented in browsers yet. In addition, using it will mean that any code using it cannot be reused between a Web Worker and non-Web Worker context.

The fundamental unit of data storage in IndexedDB is the *database*. A database in IndexedDB is roughly comparable to a database in a relational product like MySQL. Each IndexedDB database contains one or more *object stores*, which can be considered equivalent to tables in a SQL database. However, unlike a SQL database, an object store has no fixed schema.

Each record in an object store is a key/value pair, where the key is the primary index and the value is a JavaScript object. Any JavaScript object that can be serialized can be inserted into the object store.

> Closures and functions in general cannot be stored in IndexedDB.

The first step in using IndexedDB is to create a new database. To do that, just pick a name and request that it be opened. If the database does not exist, it will be created. If it does exist, it will be opened. The jQuery IndexedDB plug-in makes this easy: just name the database:

```
$.indexeddb(db);
```

After opening a database, you need to create a transaction object. The call creating this object will take a list of object stores to be used, as well as an optional mode variable and timeout. The mode variable can be `IDBTransaction.READ_ONLY`, `IDBTransaction.READ_WRITE`, or `IDBTransaction.VERSION_CHANGE`, the default being

`IDBTransaction.READ_ONLY`. The timeout is specified in milliseconds, or can be set to zero for no timeout.

The jQuery IndexedDB API implicitly creates a transaction for a simple operation, so creating an explicit transaction object as in Example 5-3 will be needed only if a change involves more than one object store or is doing something else strange. It may also be used when iterating over a list of items to add with `map`, `forEach`, or the like, to make sure all the data goes into the store in a consistent manner. When you finish with a transaction, call `transaction.done()` to commit it or `transaction.abort()` to roll it back.

Example 5-3. Using an explicit transaction

```
var transaction = $.indexeddb(db).transaction([], IDBTransaction.READ_WRITE);
transaction.then(write, writeError);
data.map(function (line){
    transaction.objectStore(objectStore).add(line).then(write, writeError);
    return line;
});
transaction.done();
```

Adding and Updating Records

All data being added to an IndexedDB database must be done inside a transaction. This protects the change from other JavaScript processes that may try to modify that same data. Even though JavaScript is single-threaded, it is possible to open the data store from a Web Worker or from a second window in the same browser so that both would be able to modify data at the same time.

In general, to add a record to a store, call the `add()` method on the object store as shown in Example 5-4. The transaction will be created automatically.

Example 5-4. Adding one line of data

```
$.indexeddb(db).objectStore(objectStore).add(book).then(wrap, err);
```

If you are adding a bunch of data, use a transaction as in Example 5-5. When all actions are done the transaction will commit. A transaction can be marked as done by calling the `transaction.done()` method, which will commit everything.

Example 5-5. Adding multiple lines of data

```
var transaction = $.indexeddb(db).transaction([], IDBTransaction.READ_WRITE);
transaction.then(write, writeError);
data.map(function (record){
    transaction.objectStore(objectStore).add(record).then(write, writeError);
});
```

To update a record, use the `update` method, which works just like the `add` method, except that it will fail if the record does not already exist.

To update a number of records at once, a cursor (see "Retrieving Data" on page 65) can be used to iterate over a group of records. In this case, call the `updateEach` method of the cursor with a callback function. This function will be called with each element from the cursor. The function should return the new value of the record, which will be saved to the database after all the records have been processed. Lines for which a false value are returned will not be saved.

Adding Indexes

Indexes can be added or removed only in a `setVersion` transaction. An index can be created when a store is created, or later with the `index()` method (see Example 5-6). This method will create the index if it does not exist. It will also return an index object that can be used to iterate over the index.

Example 5-6. Using an index

```
$.indexeddb(db).objectStore(objectStore).index(field).openCursor([1,10]).each(write);
```

One key difference between a data store like IndexedDB and most other forms of data storage is that IndexedDB runs on the customer's browser, so updating it requires a little more thought than a data storage mechanism that runs on a small set of servers in a central location. The JavaScript code must be able to cope with the possibility that the user may have an out-of-date store and update on the fly.

It is possible to check the current version of a store on a customer's computer and, if needed, bring it up to the current version. For example, version 1.0 of the software may have two stores, while in version 1.1 a third store has been added, as well as a new index in one of the original tables. By checking the version, your code can know if it should apply any needed updates or if the user's data store is set up correctly. The jQuery IndexedDB plug-in handles this automatically.

Retrieving Data

After data has been added to an object store, there must be a way to query and display it. There are several ways of interest to query data. The program may wish to display all the data, a subset of the data, or just one row.

To retrieve one row, identified by its primary key, use the `get` method as shown in Example 5-7. This method returns a promise object which is accessed via the `then` method. The `then` takes two functions as callbacks: the first is called on success with the object from the database, and the second, in case of error, with an error object.

Example 5-7. Get one row

```
$.indexeddb(db).objectStore(objectStore).get(primaryKey).then(wrap, err);
```

It's also pretty easy to query the database on an index for a single record or a range. Specify an index and then open a cursor with openCursor, specifying a range. Ranges can be inclusive or exclusive on both ends. The general form of a query is shown in Example 5-8.

Example 5-8. Get a range of rows

```
$.indexeddb(db).objectStore(objectStore).index('title').openCursor([MIN,MAX]).each(write);
```

A range is set by a four-element array in the form [lower, upper, lowerExclusive, upperExclusive]. The first two elements are integers and the second two, which are optional, are Booleans. A range is exclusive by default, so saying [10,20] will give you values of 11–19. But [10, 20, false, false] will include the end points in the search.

To search with just an upper or lower bound, leave the other parameter undefined. So [10, undefined, false] will give all keys with a value of 10 and greater, whereas [undefined, 10, undefined, true] will give all keys less than 10. To specify one value, issue something like [10, 10, false, false].

The final case comes in when one wants the entire contents of a store. Here indexes don't matter (unless they are needed for sorting), so calling openCursor on the store itself is fine. The write callback in Example 5-9 will be called on each element in turn.

Example 5-9. Get all rows

```
$.indexeddb(db).objectStore(objectStore).openCursor().each(write);
```

Deleting Data

Deleting data from an object store is also pretty easy. Each object store has a remove() method that can be called with the ID of the item to be deleted. The store will then delete that item and call the callback, as shown in Example 5-10.

Example 5-10. Deleting data

```
$.indexeddb(db).objectStore(objectStore).remove(id).then(write, err);
```

You can iterate over a cursor and delete selected rows with the deleteEach() method. This method will act similar to an array filter, deleting only those items for which the function returns true. For instance, Example 5-11 deletes all records for which the function isDuplicate() returns true.

Example 5-11. Deleting multiple items of data

```
$.indexeddb(db).objectStore(objectStore).openCursor().deleteEach(function (value, key)
                        {
                            return isDuplicate(value);
                        });
```

CHAPTER 6

Files

For obvious reasons, the browser has historically had very limited ability to access the filesystem. HTML forms have been able to upload files, and certain HTTP headers make it possible for a user to download files from the server. But outside of those specific features, the browser has not been able to access files on the local filesystem. In general this is a good thing. I don't want every web page I visit to be able to look around my hard drive!

Some of the new features of HTML5 give the browser limited access to the filesystem. Newer browsers allow JavaScript to access the files via the exiting form file input. Historically, a browser could upload a file from a form, but now it is possible to use the data from the file directly in JavaScript. In addition, the browser now lets you drag files from your desktop to a web application. Google's Gmail uses this feature to allow the user to attach files. This had been done with Flash previously, but now can be done with just JavaScript.

This does not create any new security problems, because the application already had access to this data by uploading it to the server, then downloading it again into the browser.

As of this writing, these features are supported in Firefox, Chrome, and Opera. For Safari and Internet Explorer, the Flash plug-in will work to allow file drag-and-drop.

Blobs

JavaScript has always been good at working with strings and numbers, but binary data has never been its strong point. Recently, however, it added a blob data type and interfaces to work with blobs (binary large objects). JavaScript sees a blob as a big chunk of raw data. So the amount of actual manipulation that JavaScript can do on a blob is actually somewhat limited. However, blobs are very important for moving binary data around. Blobs can be read from and written to files (see "Working with Files" on page 69), used as URLs, saved in IndexedDB (see Chapter 5), and passed to and from a Web Worker (see Chapter 8).

You can create a new blob with the BlobBuilder interface. This creates a basic empty BlobBuilder, to which is it possible to append a string, an existing blob, or binary data from an ArrayBuffer. The BlobBuilder.getBlob() method returns the actual blob.

BlobBuilder is called MozBlobBuilder in Firefox, as of version 6, and WebKitBlob Builder in Safari Nightly builds and Chrome as of version 8.

In Example 6-1, raw PNG data is passed to a BlobBuilder object to create a blob that is then turned into a URL. The URL object can be set at the src attribute of an image tag to display in the DOM.

Example 6-1. Creating a blob URL from raw data

```
/*global window, $, BlobBuilder, document, XMLHttpRequest */
/*jslint onevar: false, white: false */

function makePNG(pngData)
{
  var BlobBuilder = window.BlobBuilder || window.MozBlobBuilder ||
                    window.WebKitBlobBuilder;

  var blob = new BlobBuilder();
  blob.append(pngData);
  var url = blob.getBlob('image/png').createObjectURL();
  return url;
}
```

You can extract a section of the blob with the slice() method. Because slice has different parameters from the array and string methods of the same name, it has been renamed to mozSlice() on Firefox and webkitSlice() on Chrome. Whatever name the browser requires, the method returns the extracted data as a new blob. Taking a slice is the only access that the blob API allows to the raw data of the blob.

If a blob contains data that needs to be loaded as if it were a URL, it can be turned into something that can be used as a URL with the createObjectURL() method. This returns an object that can be assigned to an HTML tag attribute that expects a URL. For example, a blob that contains image data can be assigned to the src attribute of an <img> tag to display the image.

When done with a URL, it is important to deallocate it manually, because JavaScript will not be able to determine when to garbage-collect this object. To do this, use the revokeBlobURL() method. Blob URLs have the same origin as the creating script, so they can be used pretty flexibly in places where the browser's same-origin policy can be a problem. The browser will also revoke all blob URLs when the user navigates away from the page.

Working with Files

For many years, HTML forms have been able to include a file type as a form element that allows the user to specify a file to upload to the server. The browser does not allow JavaScript to set this field, for fear that it could somehow force the upload of a file it shouldn't. However, new JavaScript APIs allow you to read the contents of files from the local system that have been added to the form element by the user.

If you have a form with a file upload field, it will provide a `FileList` object. Each element of the `FileList` object is a `File` object. A `file` object provides the user with the file's name, MIME type, size, and last modified date. The full path is not exposed in JavaScript, but it can be seen in Firebug.

The file pointed to by a `File` object can be read in full by the `FileReader` object, or in sections by using the `.slice()` method. To upload a very large file, such as a video, it may make sense to chop the file into smaller parts and upload each part to the server instead of trying to upload a single file that may be a few hundred megabytes. It should also be noted that many servers, by default, limit file upload sizes to a few tens of megabytes.

By using the `FileReader` interface, your program can read the contents of the file. All of these methods return `void` and the data will be delivered after the browser finishes reading the file into memory, with the `onload` handler. This asynchronous operation is important because it can take some time for a very large file to be read into the browser.

The `FileReader` API has four options for reading in data:

`FileReader.readDataAsURL()`
> Transforms a file to a URL so that it can be used in the page. The resultant object will contain the full data of the file.

`FileReader.readAsText()`
> Returns the data as a string. By default, the text is encoded as UTF-8, but you can specify a different format.

`FileReader.readAsBinaryString()`
> Returns the data as a binary string, with no attempt to interpret the contents.

`FileReader.readAsArrayBuffer()`
> Returns the data as an `ArrayBuffer`.

Example 6-2 shows an example of a drop handler. Drag-and-drop file handling will be introduced fully in "Drag-and-Drop" on page 71. For now, the concepts to take away from this example are that `drop` is the name of the event passed to `addEventListener` along with a callback function, and that the function is called by the event handler with a list of files in the form of a `FileList` object. In this example, the function displays the first file in the list by creating a URL on the fly and adding it to an `<img>` tag.

Example 6-2. Appending an image to a document

```
var el = document.getElementById('dropzone');
el.addEventListener('drop', function (evt) {
    var file = evt.dataTransfer.file[0];
    file.readDataAsURL();
    file.onload = function (img)
    {
        $('div.images').append('<img>').attr({src: img});
    };
});
```

Uploading Files

Being able to drag a file from the desktop to the browser is a nice trick, but for this to really be useful you need to upload the file to the server. Newer versions of the XMLHttpRequest interface provide a way to do just that. Using the FormData interface, a program can wrap up files and send them to the server. XMLHttpRequest also provides a few callbacks where you can offer feedback to the user. An onprogress event returns the number of bytes that have been sent and the total size of the upload, which can let you display a progress bar during large uploads. An oncomplete event is fired when the upload is finished.

When you upload files with XMLHttpRequest, the server will see the upload in the same interfaces that would be used with a standard <input type='file' multiple> form interface. So the server-side code for this should be the same standard code for file uploads that has been in use since the form element was introduced.

Example 6-3 shows an example of code to upload files over Ajax. It uses the FormData object to wrap up the files, which are then sent to the server. FormData is a JavaScript object that can package data as a file upload so that a standard HTTP upload can be performed. To do this, pass the filename and the file as a blob to FormData.append(). Then, using the XHR2 interface, send the FormData object to the server as the Ajax payload.

Example 6-3. Uploading files with Ajax

```
function upload(files){
var uploadBlob = function uploadBlob(files, onload) {
    var xhr = new XMLHttpRequest();
    xhr.open('POST', params.url, true);
    xhr.onload = onload;
    xhr.send(files);
};

var formData = new FormData();
files.map(function (file) {
    formData.append(file.fileName, file);
    return file;
});
```

```
uploadBlob(files, function (){
    alert("Upload Finished");

    });
    }
```

Drag-and-Drop

HTML5 has increased support for drag-and-drop. It is now possible to drag and drop one or more files from the desktop to the browser and give JavaScript access to the contents of those files. This could be used, for example, by a file manager to upload files to a server, or by a graphics program to manipulate images. A social networking site could allow a user to drag images to your browser, and then crop, scale, rotate, and preview them in the browser before uploading them to the server. This could save server resources by providing it with smaller images.

 The File APIs, for security reasons, will not let you upload a directory structure, but just a list of simple files. If you are building a file manager, you can of course have the user upload an archive file (*ZIP*, *RAR*, *tar*, etc.) and have the server expand it. There are libraries to unpack most archive formats in most of the popular server-side languages.

To implement drag-and-drop, add a listener to the **drop** event of the DOM element that is the drop target. The event handler you specify will be passed an argument that will have a list in it that contains all of the files that have been dragged. Note that this object looks like an array, in that it has numeric keys and a length property. However, it is not actually an array, and trying to call **map** or any of the other array operators on it will not work.

 Selenium can't drag a file from the desktop to the browser, so there is no way to automatically test drag-and-drop with Selenium.

Putting It All Together

To show how the features described in this chapter work together for a convenient file handling interface, this section presents a more complete example (Example 6-4), designating an area of the web page as a drop zone. After the user drops a file, it is packaged with the `FormData` object and uploaded via the `XMLHttpRequest` object. The function also shows a progress indicator to give the user feedback about what is happening.

Example 6-4. Uploading files

```
/*global $, FormData,alert, document, XMLHttpRequest */
/*jslint onevar: false, white: false */


(function () {
    var toArray = function toArray(files) {
        var output = [];
        for (var i = 0, f; f = files[i]; i += 1) {
            output.push(f);
        }
        return output;
    };

    var updateProgress = function (state) {
        var progress = $('progress#progress');
        progress.attr('max', 100);
        if (state === 'start') {
            return progress.fadeIn(500);
        }
        else if (state === 'stop') {
            return progress.fadeOut(500);
        }
        // use the jQuery UI Progress bars
        return progress.attr('value', state);
    };

    var uploadBlob = function uploadBlob(params) {
        var xhr = new XMLHttpRequest();
        xhr.open('POST', params.url, true);
        xhr.onload = params.success;

        // Listen to the upload progress.
        xhr.upload.onprogress = params.progress;

        xhr.send(params.blob);
        return params;
    };


    var fileupload = function fileupload() {

        var el = document.getElementById('dropzone');
        var stopEvent = function (evt) {
            evt.stopPropagation();
            evt.preventDefault();
        };
        el.addEventListener('dragover', stopEvent, false);

        el.addEventListener('drop', function (evt) {
            stopEvent(evt);

            var files = toArray(evt.dataTransfer.files);

            updateProgress('start');
```

```
        var packageFiles = function (files) {
            var formData = new FormData();
            files.map(function (file) {
                formData.append(file.fileName, file);
                return file;
            });

            var block = {
                url: '/upload.php',
                success: function () {
                    updateProgress('done');
                },
                progress: function (evt) {
                    updateProgress(100 * (evt.loaded / evt.total));
                },
                blob: formData
            };
            return block;
        };
        uploadBlob(packageFiles(files));
    }, false);
};
//run setup
fileupload();
}());
```

At the beginning I create a function named **toArray** that packs filenames into an array. The following **updateProgress** function uses a new progress bar provided by HTML5, described in "Tags for Applications" on page 111. The **uploadBlob** function repeats the code shown in Example 6-3. The **fileupload** function also uses some of that code in addition to code from Example 6-2.

Filesystem

The idea of a browser allowing JavaScript to access the filesystem is enough to send anyone who thinks about security into a panic. There are many things on any user's hard drive that one would not want the browser to be able to access.

Google Chrome allows JavaScript to access a sandboxed filesystem on the user's computer. If you want to run the FileSystem API from inside a web page, Chrome must be started with the `--unlimited-quota-for-files` flag. However, if you are building an app for the Google Web Store you can access this API by specifying `unlimitedStorage` in the store manifest file.

While **localStorage** and IndexedDB allow a JavaScript program to store objects in a database, the FileSystem API is useful for storing large binary objects. For example, if you're building a video app, it may be useful to store working images on a filesystem. Other use cases could include streaming video, games with lots of media assets, image editing, or audio applications. In short, this interface will be a good fit for any application that needs to store a lot of data locally, on a short-term or long-term basis.

 Because the FileSystem API is supported only in Chrome, and only when the user has loaded a trusted app, it is somewhat beyond the scope of this book. A full treatment can be found in the book *Using the HTML5 Filesystem API* by Eric Bidelman (O'Reilly).

CHAPTER 7

Taking It Offline

The Internet may seem to be always on these days but, let's be honest, it's not. There are times and places when even the most modern mobile devices are out of range of the network for one reason or another.

Chapter 4 looked at how to have data stored local to the browser so that it does not require network access to use. However, if the web page on which the application is hosted is not available, having the data handy will be of no use.

With more and more of the modern application infrastructure moving into the browser, being able to access this software at any time has become critically important. The problem is that the standard web application assumes that many components, including JavaScript sources, HTML, images, CSS, and so forth, will be loaded with the web page. In order to be able to use those resources when the user does not have access to the Internet requires that copies of those files be stored locally, and used by the browser when needed. HTML5 lets a programmer give the browser a listing (known as a *manifest*) of files that should be loaded and saved. The browser will be able to access these files even when there is no network connection to the server.

The files listed in the manifest will also be loaded from the local disk even if the browser is online, thus giving the end user the experience of the ultimate content delivery network.

As long as the browser is online when a page is loaded, it will check the manifest file with the server. If the manifest file has changed, the browser will attempt to redownload all the files listed for download in the manifest. Once all the files in the manifest have been downloaded, the browser will update the file cache to show the new files.

Introduction to the Manifest File

The ability to access files while offline was one of the features introduced by Google in Gears. The user provided a manifest as a JSON file, which then directed the browser to load other required files offline. When the browser next visited that page, the files would be loaded from the local disk instead of from the network. When the version field of the manifest file was updated, Gears would check all the files in the manifest for updates.

The HTML5 manifest is similar in idea but somewhat different in implementation. One nice thing about it is that you can implement a manifest in an application without using any JavaScript code, which Gears did require. To create a manifest, add the `manifest` attribute containing the name of the manifest file to the document's `<html>` tag (see Example 7-1).

Example 7-1. HTML manifest declaration

```
<!DOCTYPE HTML>
<html manifest="/cache.manifest">
<body>
      ...
</body>
</html>
```

The manifest file must be served with the MIME type `text/cache-manifest`. This can be done via the web server configuration files. For the Apache web server, add the following line to the config file. For other web servers, consult the server's documentation. The filename does not matter as long as the file has the correct MIME type, but `cache.manifest` seems to be a good default choice:

```
AddType text/cache-manifest  .manifest
```

Structure of the Manifest File

The format of the manifest file is in fact pretty simple. The first line must be just the words `CACHE MANIFEST`. After that comes a list of files, one per line, to include in the manifest (see Example 7-2). Comments can be marked with the pound (#) character.

The manifest will cache `HTTP GET` requests, while `POST`, `PUT`, and `DELETE` will still go to the network. If the page has an active manifest file, all `GET` requests will be directed to local storage. But for some files, offline access does not make sense. These can include various server resources such as Ajax calls, or collections of documents that could get so large as to overflow the cache area. These files can be included in a `NETWORK` section of the manifest. Any URLs in the `NETWORK` section will bypass the cache and load directly from the server. The HTML5 manifest specification requires that any non-included files be explicitly opted out of the manifest.

In other cases, you may wish to provide different content depending on whether the user is offline or online. The manifest provides a `FALLBACK` section for such resources. The user will be shown different content, depending on whether the browser has a connection to the Internet or not. On each line of the `FALLBACK` section, the first file is loaded from the server when a connection is available, and the second file is loaded locally when the connection is not available.

Both the NETWORK and FALLBACK sections list file patterns, not specific files. So it is possible to list entire directories or URL paths here, as well as file types such as images (e.g., *.jpg).

Example 7-2. Manifest file

```
CACHE MANIFEST
# 11 October 2010
/index.php
/js/jquery.js
/css/style.css
/images/logo.png

NETWORK:
/request.php

FALLBACK:
/about.html /offline-about.html
```

Updates to the Manifest File

The browser will update the files in the manifest whenever the manifest file itself changes. There are several ways to handle this. It is possible to add a version number in a comment in the file. If the project is making use of a version control system like Subversion, you can use the version number tag for this.

The problem with using a version number from a version control system is that it requires a programmer to remember to update that file every time any file in the system changes. It would be much better to create an automated system that updates the manifest file whenever a file listed in it changes, and run that script as part of a deployment procedure.

For instance, you could write a script that checks all the files in the manifest for changes and then change the manifest file itself when one of the files changes. A simple way to do this is to write a script that loops over all the files in the manifest, then does an MD5 checksum on each one, then puts a final checksum into the manifest file. This will ensure that any changes will cause the manifest file to update.

This script is probably too slow to run from the web server, as running it hundreds of times a second would be overkill. However, it can be efficiently run in the development environment. One option would be to have it run from an editor when a file is saved. Another option is to run it as part of the check-in process for a version control system.

In Example 7-3, we parse the manifest file and do a few things with it. The program uses the Symfony Yaml Library (*http://components.symfony-project.org/yaml*) to load a list of files to use as a manifest. As a bonus, the program first checks that no file has been included more than once. It also checks that every file exists, because missing files will break the manifest. By adding each file's MD5 as a comment after the filename, the script makes sure that any updated file will cause a manifest change so that the browser will update its content. It takes a datafile in the format of Example 7-5. Example 7-3 will output a manifest file with the MD5 hash as a comment in the file, as in Example 7-4.

Example 7-3. Automatically updating a manifest file

```php
<?php

header('Content-Type: text/cache-manifest');
echo ("CACHE MANIFEST\n");
$files = sfYaml::load('manifest.yml');
$hashes = '';
$files = unique($files);

foreach($files->cache as $file)
  {
    if(file_exists($file))
      {
      echo $file."\n";
      $hashes .=md5_file($file);
      }
  }
echo "\nnNETWORK:\n"
foreach ($files->network as $file)
{
  echo $file. "\n";
}

echo "\nFALLBACK:\n"
foreach ($files->fallback as $file)
{
  echo $file. "\n";
}

echo "# HASH: ". md5($hashes) . "\n";
```

Example 7-4. Manifest with MD5 hash

```
CACHE MANIFEST
index.html
css/style.js
js/jquery.js
js/myscript.js

NETWORK:
network/file

FALLBACK:
/avatars/ /offline-avatars/offline.png

#HASH: 090c7e8fe42c16777fba844f835e839b
```

Example 7-5. The data for Example 7-3

```
files:
  - index.html
  - css/style.css
  - js/jquery.js
  - js/myscript.js

network:
  - network/file

faillback:
  - /avatars/ /offline-avatars/offline.png
```

 The manifest is not always very good about updating when you think it should. Even with a new version of a manifest, it can often take some time to update the content in the browser. Unless you set the cache control headers, the browser will not download the manifest again until several hours after it was last downloaded. Make sure the cache control headers don't cause the browser to only download the file, say, every five years, or use the ETag header. Or, better yet, have the server set a no cache header. Be sure to test well.

Events

When the browser loads a page with a manifest file, it will fire a `checking` event on the `window.applicationCache` object. This event will fire whether or not the page has been visited before.

If the cache has not been seen before, the browser will fire a `downloading` event, and start to download the files. This event will also fire if the manifest file has changed. If the manifest has not changed the browser will fire a `noupdate` event.

As the browser downloads the files, it fires a series of `progress` events. These can be used if you wish to provide some form of feedback to the user to let her know that software is downloading.

Once all the files have downloaded, the `cached` event is fired.

If anything goes wrong, the browser will fire the `error` event. This can be caused by a problem in the HTML page, a defective manifest, or a failure to download the manifest or any resource listed in it. Normally, if a single file is missing from the manifest, the cache won't download any of the files in the manifest. When a manifest changes and ends up including a bad link, the old version of the file will be retained. If there was no existing manifest at the time the erroneous manifest is downloaded, the browser will not create an incomplete offline storage, but will continue to rely on the network.

However, it is possible that not all browsers or browser versions will handle erroneous manifests in the exact way just described. Having an automatic test to validate all the URLs in a manifest is a good idea. This can be a very hard error to catch because there may be very little visible evidence of what went wrong. Catching the error object in your JavaScript and presenting it to the user would be a good idea, as would some form of automatic testing for bad links.

In Google Chrome, the Developer Tools can show a list of files in the manifest (see Figure 7-1). Under the Storage tab, the Application Cache item will show the status of various items.

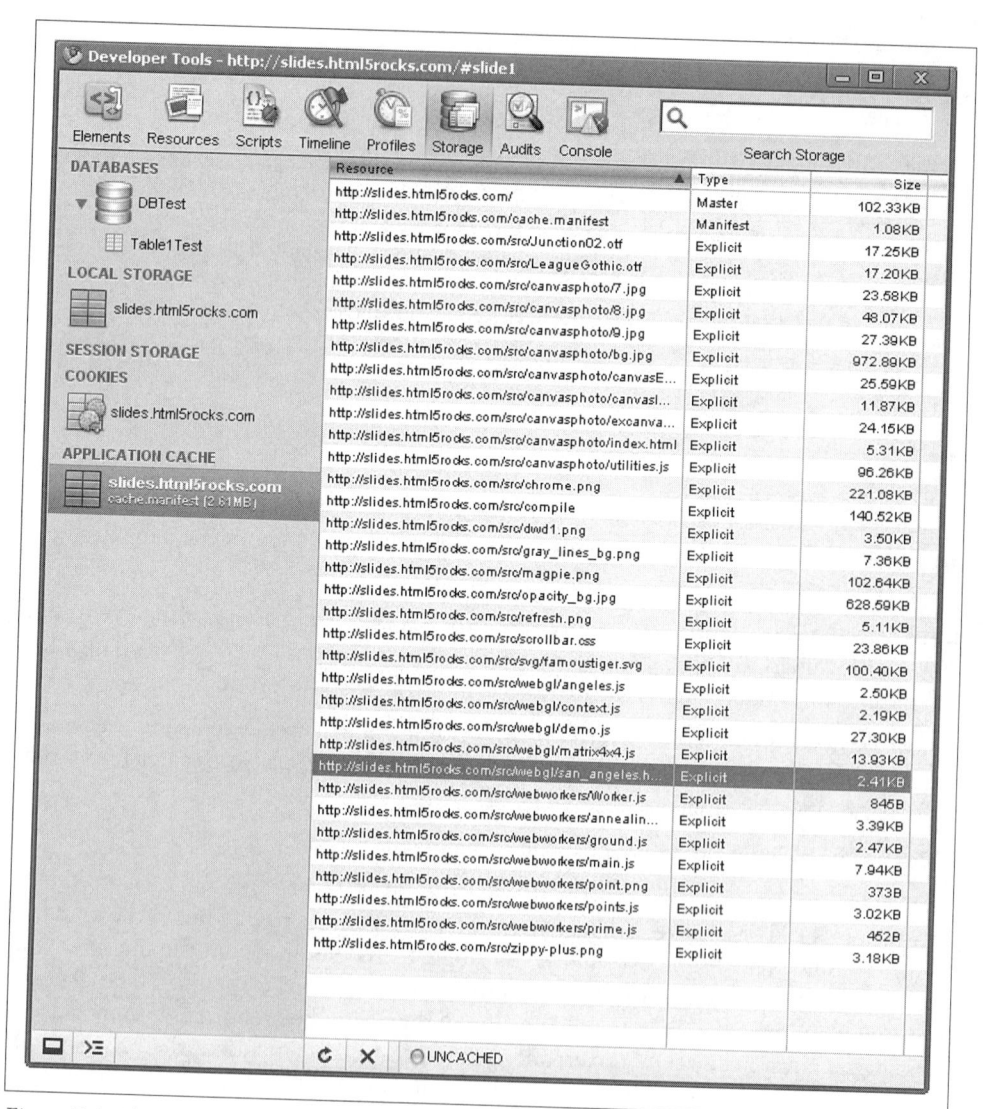

Figure 7-1. Chrome Storage Viewer showing Application Cache

 It is a good idea during development to turn off the manifest file, and enable it only when the project is ready to go live. Using the cache can make it very hard to develop the application if changes don't appear quickly.

Debugging Manifest Files

Manifest files provide a particular debugging challenge. They can be the source of several special classes of bugs.

The first and most obvious bug is to include missing files in the manifest. If a file is included in the page and it is not in the manifest, it will not be loaded by the page, in the same way a missing file on the server will not be downloaded.

Many Selenium tests will not explicitly test for correct styles and the presence of images, so it is quite possible that an application missing a CSS file or image will still work to the extent that it is normally tested in Selenium. In an application that includes resources from outside web servers, those must also be whitelisted in the manifest file.

A further complication comes in some browsers, including Firefox, that make the manifest an opt-in feature. So a Selenium test may not opt into it, which would make the entire test moot. In order to test this in Firefox, it will be necessary to set up a Firefox profile in which the application cache is on by default. To do this:

1. Quit Firefox completely.
2. Start up Firefox from a command line with the `-profileManager` switch. This will result in a dialog similar to that shown in Figure 7-2. Save the custom profile.

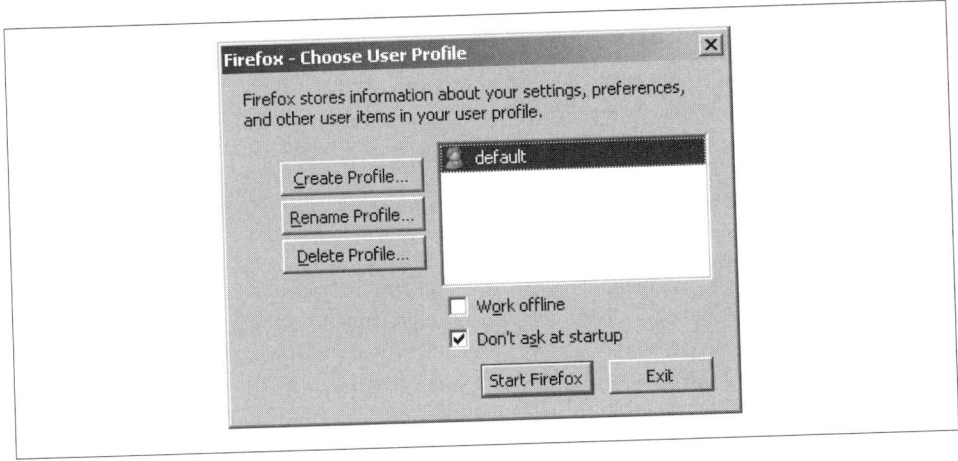

Figure 7-2. Firefox custom profile dialog

3. Restart Firefox. Go to the Firefox Options menu, select the Advanced tab and under that the Network tab (see Figure 7-3), and turn off the "Tell me when a website asks to store data for offline use" option.

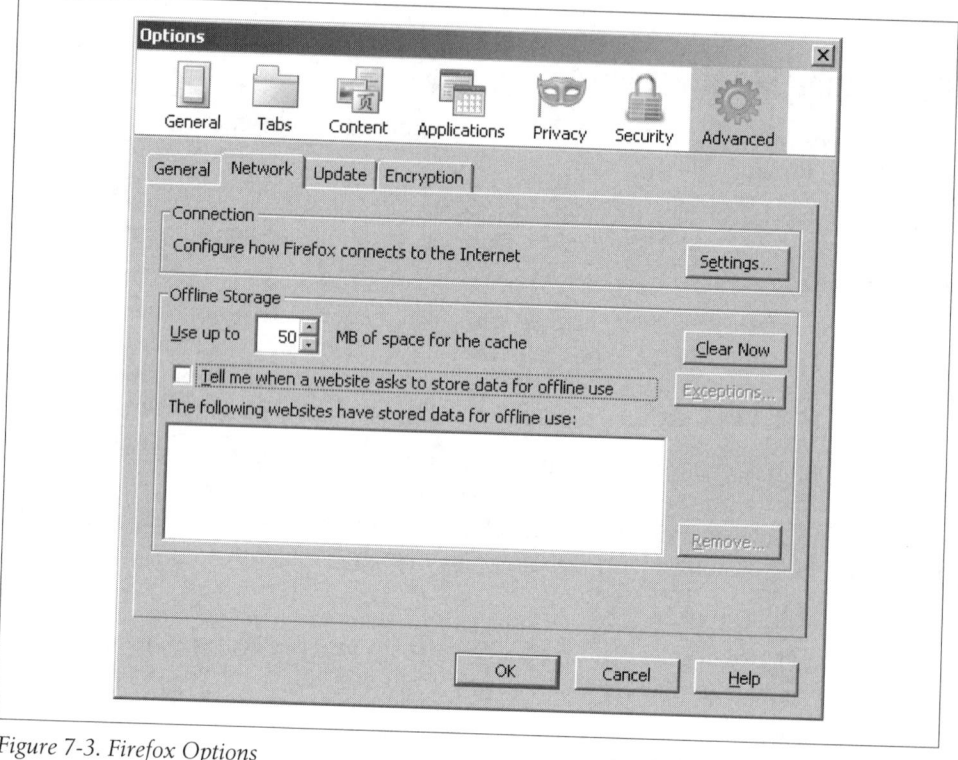

Figure 7-3. Firefox Options

Now, when starting up the Selenium RC server, use an option like this:

```
java -jar selenium-server.jar -firefoxProfileTemplate
```

For full details on Firefox profiles, see *http://support.mozilla.com/en-US/kb/Managing +profiles.*

A second class of problems can occur when the manifest is updated and the browser does not reflect the update. Normally, it will take a minute or two after loading a page for the browser to update the file cache, and the browser will not check the cache until the page is loaded. So if the server is updated, the browser will not have the new version until the user visits the page. This can cause problems if there has been an update on the server that will cause the application in the browser to fail, such as a change in the format of how data is sent between the client and server.

When the user visits the page (assuming of course that the browser is online), the browser will fetch the manifest file from the server. However, if the manifest file has a cache control header set on it, the browser may not check for a new version of the manifest. For example, if the file has a header that says the browser should check for updates only once a year (as is sometimes common on web servers), the browser will not reload the manifest file. So it is very important to ensure that the manifest file itself is not cached by the browser, or if it is cached it is done only via an ETag.

The browser can always prevent caching of the manifest file by giving the URL with a query string attached, as in `cache.manifest?load=1`. If the manifest file is a static text file, the query string will be ignored, but the browser will not know that and will force the server to send a fresh copy.

Different web browsers, and even different versions of a single browser, may update the manifest file somewhat differently. So it is very important to test any application using a manifest file very carefully across different browsers and browser versions.

CHAPTER 8

Splitting Up Work Through Web Workers

JavaScript has, since its inception, run in a single thread. With small applications this was practical, but it runs up against certain limits now, with larger and larger applications being loaded into browsers. As more and more JavaScript is run, the application will start to block, waiting for code to finish.

JavaScript runs code from an event loop that takes events off a queue of all the events that have happened in the browser. Whenever the JavaScript runtime is idle, it takes the first event off the queue and runs the handler that goes with that event (see Figure 8-1). As long as those handlers run quickly, this makes for a responsive user experience.

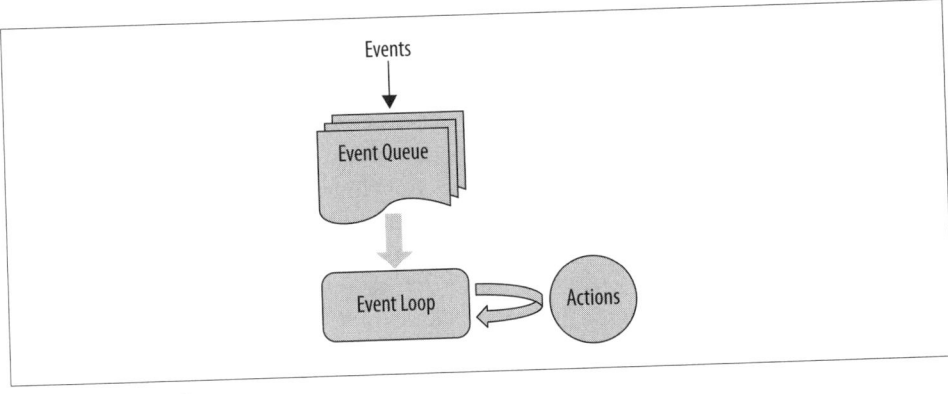

Figure 8-1. Event loop

In the past few years, the competition among browsers has in part revolved around the speed of JavaScript. In Chrome and Firefox, JavaScript can now run as much as 100 times faster than it did back in the days of IE 6. Because of this, it is possible to squeeze more into the event loop.

Thankfully, most of the things JavaScript has to do are fast. They tend to be on the order of manipulating some data and passing it into the DOM or making an Ajax call. So the model in Figure 8-1 works pretty well. For things that would take longer than a fraction of a second to compute, a number of tricks can prevent bottlenecks from affecting the user experience.

The main trick is to break the computation into small steps and run each one as an independent job on the queue. Each step ends with a call to the next step after a short delay—say, 1/100 of a second. This prevents the task from locking up the event queue. But it's still fundamentally unsatisfactory, as it puts the work of the task scheduler on to the programmer. Tuning this solution to make it effective is also a demanding effort. If the time steps are too small, computation can still clog up the event queue and cause other tasks to lag behind. So things will still happen, but the user will feel the lag as the system fails to respond right away to clicks and other user-visible activities. On the other hand, if the steps between actions are too large, the computation will take a very long time to complete, causing the user to wait for her results.

Google Gears created the idea of the "worker pool," which has turned into the HTML5 Web Worker. The interfaces are somewhat different, but the basic ideas are the same. A worker is a separate JavaScript process that can perform computations and pass messages back and forth with the main process and other workers. A Web Worker differs from a thread in Java or Python in one key aspect of design: *there is no shared state*. The workers and the main JavaScript instance can communicate only by passing messages.

That one difference leads to a number of key programming practices, most simpler than thread programming. Web Workers have no need for mutexes, locks, or synchronization. Deadlocks and race conditions can't occur. This also means you can use the huge number of JavaScript packages out there without worrying whether they are thread-safe. The only changes to the browser's JavaScript environment are a few new methods and events.

Each worker (including the main window) maintains an independent event loop. Whenever there is no code running, the JavaScript runtime returns to this event loop and takes the first message out of the queue. If there are no events in the queue, it will wait until an event arrives and then handle it. If some piece of code is running for a long time, no events will be handled until that piece of code is finished. In the main window, this will result in the browser user interface locking up. (Some browsers will offer to let you stop JavaScript at this point.) In a worker, a long task will keep the worker from accepting any new events. However, the main window, and any other workers, will continue to be responsive.

This design choice does, however, place some restrictions on the worker processes themselves. First, workers do not have access to the DOM. This also means a worker can't use the Firebug console interface, as Firebug communicates with JavaScript by way of the DOM. Finally, JavaScript debuggers cannot access workers, so there is no way to step through code or do any of the other things that would normally be done in the debugger.

Web Worker Use Cases

The types of applications traditionally run on the Web, and the limitations of the web browser environment, limited the computational needs that would call for a Web Worker. Until recently, most web applications manipulated small amounts of data consisting mostly of text and numbers. In these cases, a Web Worker type of construct is of limited use. Now JavaScript is asked to do a lot more, and many common situations can benefit from spawning new tasks.

Graphics

The HTML5 `<svg>` and `<canvas>` tags allow JavaScript to manipulate images, potentially a computationally heavy task. Although web browsers have been able to display images since the release of the Mosaic browser around 1993, the browsers couldn't manipulate those images. If a web programmer wanted to distort an image, overlay it transparently, and so forth, it could not be done in the browser. In the `<img>` tag, all the browser could do is substitute a different image by changing the `src` attribute, or change the displayed size of the image. However, the browser had no way of knowing what the image was or accessing the raw data that made up the image.

The recently added `<canvas>` tag makes it possible to import an existing image into a canvas and export the raw data back into JavaScript for processing, as long as the image was loaded from the same server as the page it is on. It is also possible to export a frame from a video in the HTML5 `<video>` tag.[*]

Once the data has been extracted from a graphic, you can pass it to a worker for post-processing. This could be useful for doing anything from cleaning up an image to doing a Fourier transform on a scientific data set. Canvas makes it possible to build complex image editing through various filters written in JavaScript, which should often use Web Workers for better performance.

---

[*] See *HTML5 Canvas* by Steve Fulton and Jeff Fulton (O'Reilly) for more information on the graphics in HTML5.

Maps

In addition to graphics, JavaScript has APIs now for handling map data. Being able to import a map from the Internet and find out the user's current location via geolocation allows a wide range of web application services.

Suppose you build a route finder into a mobile browser. It would be very nice to be able to take your phone and tell it you wish to go to "#14 King George St, Tel Aviv" and have the browser figure out where you are, direct you to the nearest bus stop, and tell you that you should take the number 82 bus to get there from the Diamond District in Ramat Gan.

An even more complex version of that software might check traffic to tell you that a different bus might take a more roundabout route and leave you a block from your destination, but probably run faster by missing a major traffic snarl.

Using Web Workers

To start up a Web Worker, create a new `Worker` object and pass, as the parameter to the call, the file that contains the code (see Example 8-1). This will create a worker from the source file.

Example 8-1. Worker example

```
$(document).ready(function (){
   var worker = new Worker('worker.js');
   worker.onmessage = function (event){
      console.info(event);
   };
   worker.postMessage("World" );
});
```

The browser will load the worker, run any code that is not in an event handler, and then launch the event loop to wait for events. The main event to be concerned with is the `message` event, which is how you send data to the worker. The main thread sends the message by issuing `postMessage()` and passing data as the argument.

The data from the main thread is held in the `event.data` field. The worker should retrieve this data through a call to `onmessage()`.

The Worker Environment

Web Workers run in a pretty minimal environment. Many of the familiar objects and interfaces of JavaScript in the browser are missing, including the DOM, the `document` object, and the `window` object.

In addition to the standard ECMAScript objects like `String`, `Array`, and `Date`, the following objects and interfaces are available to the Web Worker:

- The `navigator` object, which contains four properties: `appName`, `appVersion`, `userAgent`, and `platform`
- The `location` object, with all properties read-only
- The `self` object, which is the worker object
- The `importScripts()` method
- The `XMLHttpRequest` interface for doing Ajax methods
- `setTimeout()` and `setInterval()`
- The `close()` method, which ends the worker process

ECMAScript 5 JSON interfaces can also be used, as they are part of the language, not the browser enviroment. Furthermore, the worker can import library scripts from the server with the `importScripts()` method. This method takes a list of one or more files, which are then loaded. This has the same effect as using a `<script>` tag in the main user interface thread. Unlike most methods in JavaScript, `importScripts` is blocking. The function will not return until all the listed scripts have been loaded. `importScripts` will execute the loaded files in the order in which they were specified to the command.

Although `localStorage` and `sessionStorage` are not accessible from the Web Worker, IndexedDB databases are (see Chapter 5). In addition, the IndexedDB specification says that the blocking forms of calls can be used in a Web Worker (but not in the main window). So if you want a worker to manipulate data through IndexedDB, it would make sense to load the new data into the database and then send an "updated" message to the main window or other workers so that they can take any needed actions.

Worker Communication

The main event that concerns a worker is the `message` event, which is sent to the worker from the `postMessage` method in the main JavaScript context to pass information. In Firefox, it is possible to pass complex JavaScript objects. However, some versions of Chrome and Safari support only simple data, such as strings, Booleans, and numbers. It is good practice to encode all data into JSON before sending it to a Web Worker.

The worker can send data back to the main thread via the same `postMessage` method, and receive it back in the main thread via the `worker.onmessage` handler.

The model for worker communication is that the main task creates the worker, after which they pass messages back and forth as shown in Figure 8-2.

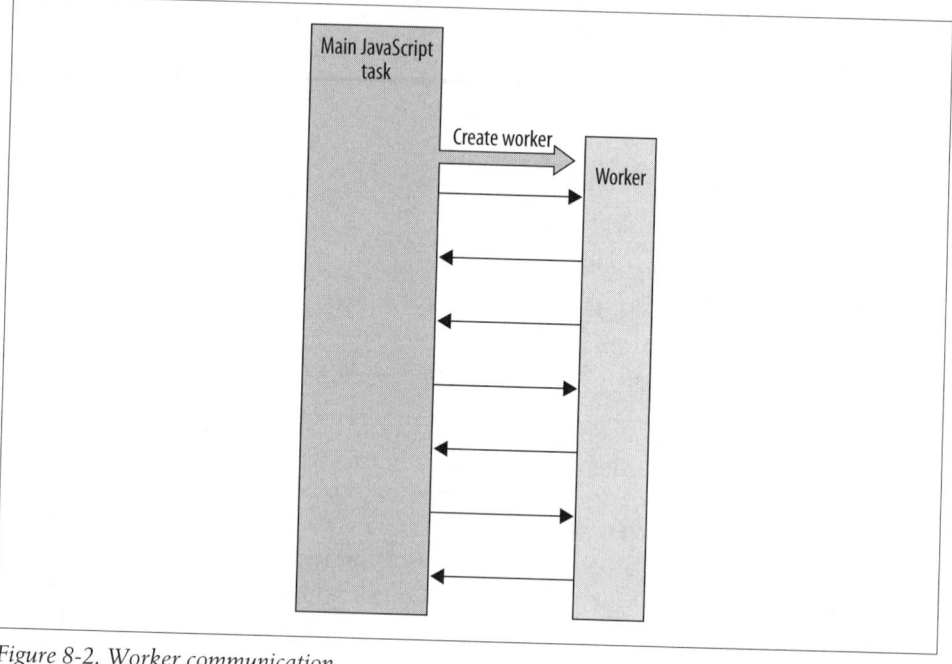

Figure 8-2. Worker communication

Web Worker Fractal Example

Example 8-1 is the "Hello World" of Web Workers. A more complex example is called for. Figure 8-3 shows a visual representation of a Mandelbrot set computed in a Web Worker. Here the worker and the main thread split up the work to draw the fractal. The worker does the actual work of computing the Mandelbrot set, while the frontend script takes that raw data and displays it in the canvas.

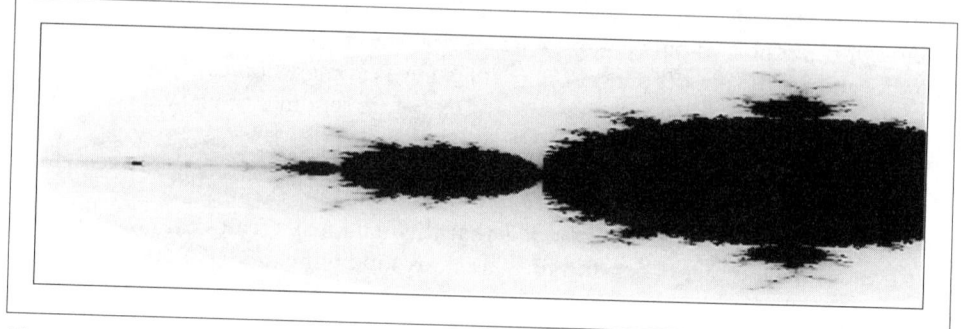

Figure 8-3. Mandelbrot example

The frontend script (see Example 8-2) sets up the canvas element and scales it to fit in the page. Then it creates an object to wrap the worker interface. The wrapper object creates the worker in the wrapper's `run()` method, passing to the worker a parameter block that tells it what chunk of the Mandelbrot set to compute.

The `draw` method takes the data, scales it to fit onto the canvas, sets a color, and then draws the pixel.

 The HTML Canvas does not have a "draw pixel" command, so to draw a pixel we must draw a square of size 1 and offset it by half a pixel from the spot where we want it to show up. So to draw a pixel at (20,20) the square should extend from (19.5,19.5) to (20.5,20.5). The locations on the canvas grid are not the pixels on the screen but the points between them.

The `onmessage` handler then waits for events to be sent from the worker. If the event type is `draw`, the handler calls the method to draw the new data into the canvas. If the event is `log`, it is logged to the JavaScript console via `console.info()`. This provides a very simple method to log status information from a worker.

The `startWorker` method aliases the `this` to a local variable named `that`. This is because `this` is not lexically scoped like other JavaScript variables. To allow the inner function to have access to that object, which it will need to draw a pixel, it is necessary to alias it to a lexically scoped variable. By convention that variable is often called `that`.

Example 8-2. Mandelbrot frontend

```
var drawMandelSet = function drawMandelSet(){

    var mandelPanel = $('body');

    var width = mandelPanel.innerWidth();
    var height = mandelPanel.innerHeight();

    var range = [{
        x: -2,
        y: -1.4
    }, {
        x: 5,
        y: 1.4
    }];

    $('canvas#fractal').height(height + 100);
    $('canvas#fractal').width(width  - 50);
    var left = 0;
    var top = 0;

    var canvas = $("canvas#fractal")[0];
    var ctx = canvas.getContext("2d");
    var params = {
```

```
            range: range,
            startx: 0.0,
            starty: 0.0,
            width: width,
            height: height
        };
        var y_array = [];

        var worker = {
            params: params,

            draw: function draw(data){
                data.forEach(function d(point){
                    if (this.axis.x[point.drawLoc.x] === undefined) {
                        this.axis.x[point.drawLoc.x] = point.point.x;
                    }
                    if (this.axis.y[height - point.drawLoc.y] === undefined) {
                        this.axis.y[height - point.drawLoc.y] = point.point.y;
                    }

                    ctx.fillStyle = pickColor(point.escapeValue);
                    ctx.fillRect(point.drawLoc.x + 0.5,
                                height - point.drawLoc.y + 0.5, 1, 1);
                }, this);
            },

            axis: {
                x: [],
                y: [],
                find: function(x, y){
                    return new Complex(this.x[x], this.y[y]);
                },

                reset: function(){
                    this.x = [], this.y = [];
                }
            },
            myWorker: false,

            run: function startWorker(params){
                this.myWorker = new Worker("js/worker.js");

                var that = this;
                this.myWorker.postMessage(JSON.stringify(params));

                this.myWorker.onmessage = function(event){

                    var data = JSON.parse(event.data);
                    if (data.type === 'draw') {
                        that.draw(JSON.parse(data.data));
                    }
                    else
                        if (event.data.type === 'log') {
                            console.info(event);
                        }
```

```
                };
            }
        };

    worker.run(params);
    return worker;
};


$(document).ready(drawMandelSet);

Function.prototype.createDelegate = function createDelegate(scope){
    var fn = this;
    return function(){
        fn.call(scope, arguments);
    };
};

function pickColor(escapeValue){
    if (escapeValue === Complex.prototype.max_iteration) {
        return "black";
    }

    var tone = 255 - escapeValue * 10;
    var colorCss = "rgb({r},{g},{b})".populate({
        r: tone,
        g: tone,
        b: tone
    });
    return colorCss;
}

String.prototype.populate = function populate(params) {
    var str = this.replace(/\{\w+\}/g, function stringFormatInner(word) {
        return params[word.substr(1, word.length - 2)];
    });
    return str;
};
```

The actual worker (see Example 8-3) is very simple. It just loads up a few other files and then waits for a message to be sent from the user interface. When it gets one, it starts the computation.

Example 8-3. Mandelbrot startup

```
importScripts('function.js','json2.js', 'complex.js','computeMandelbrot.js',
            'buildMaster.js');

onmessage = function(event){
    var data = typeof event.data === 'string'? JSON.parse(event.data) :  event.data;
    buildMaster(data);
};
```

The buildMaster() function (see Example 8-4) loops over the grid of points for the Mandelbrot set, computing the escape value for each point (see Example 8-5). After

every 200 points, the build function sends the results of its computation back to the
main thread for drawing, and then zeros out its internal buffer of computed points.
This way, instead of waiting for the entire grid to be drawn at once, the user sees the
image build progressively.

Example 8-4. Mandelbrot build

```
var chunkSize = 200;
function buildMaster(data){

    var range = data.range;
    var width = data.width;
    var height = data.height;
    var startx = data.startx;
    var starty = data.starty;
    var dx = (range[1].x - range[0].x) / width;
    var dy = (range[1].y - range[0].y) / height;


    function send(line){
        var lineData = JSON.stringify(line.map(function makeReturnData(point){
            return {
                drawLoc: point.drawLoc,
                point: point.point,
                escapeValue: point.point.mandelbrot()
            };
        }));

        var json = JSON.stringify({
            type: 'draw',
            data: lineData
        });
        postMessage(json);
    };


    function xIter(x, maxX, drawX){
        var line = [];
        var drawY = starty;
        var y = range[0].y;
        var maxY = range[1].y;

        while (y < maxY) {
            if (line.length % chunkSize === chunkSize - 1) {
                send(line);
                line = [];

            }
            var pt = {
                point: new Complex(x, y),
                drawLoc: {
                    x: drawX,
                    y: drawY
                }
            };
```

```
                line.push(pt);
                y += dy;
                drawY += 1;
            }
            send(line);
            if (x < maxX && drawX < width) {
                xIter.defer(1, this, [x + dx, maxX, drawX + 1]);
            }
        }
    }

    xIter(range[0].x, range[1].x, startx);

}
```

The final part of this application is the actual mathematical computation of the Mandelbrot set shown in Example 8-5. This function is done as a while loop instead of a pure function as in "Functional Programming" on page 13, because JavaScript does not support tail recursion. Doing this as a recursive function would be more elegant, but would risk causing a stack overflow.

Example 8-5. Mandelbrot computation

```
Complex.prototype.max_iteration = 255 * 2;
Complex.prototype.mandelbrot = function(){

    var x0 = this.x;
    var y0 = this.y;
    var x = x0;
    var y = y0;
    var count;
    var x_, y_;
    var max_iteration = this.max_iteration;
    function inSet(x, y){
        return x * x + y * y < 4;
    }
    count = 0;
    while (count < max_iteration && inSet(x, y)) {
        x_ = x * x - y * y + x0;
        y_ = 2 * x * y + y0;
        count += 1;
        x = x_;
        y = y_;
    }

    return count;
};
```

While the worker is doing the calculation of the Mandelbrot set, its main event is blocked. So it is not possible for the UI process to send it a new computation task, or more correctly stated, the worker will not accept the new task until the current task is finished.

To interrupt or change a worker's behavior—for instance, to let the user in the user interface thread select which area of the Mandelbrot set to draw and then request that the worker draw that area—you have a choice among a few methods.

The simplest method would be to kill the worker and create a new one. This has the advantage that the new worker starts off on a clean state and there can be nothing left over from the prior runs. On the other hand, it also means the worker has to load all the scripts and data from scratch. So if the worker has a long startup time, this is probably not the best approach.

The second method is a little more complex: manage the task queue manually through your program. Have a data structure in the main thread or a worker that keeps a list of blocks of data to compute. When a worker needs a task, it can send a message to that queue object and have a task sent to it. This creates more complexity but has several advantages. First, the worker does not need to be restarted when the application needs it to do something different. Second, it allows the use of multiple workers. Each worker can query the queue manager when it needs the next part of the problem.

You could also have the master task send a large number of events to the worker in sequence. However, this has the problem that there is no way from JavaScript to clear the event queue. So having a job queue that can be managed seems to be the best approach. We'll explore this solution in the following section.

There is no requirement that an application restrict itself to one Web Worker. JavaScript is quite happy to let you start up a reasonable number of workers. Of course, this makes sense only if the problem can be easily partitioned into several workers, but many problems can be divided that way.

Each worker is an independent construction, so it is possible to create several workers from the same source code, or to create several workers that work independently.

Workers are a fairly heavy construct in JavaScript, so it is probably a bad idea to create more than, say, 10 workers on a given task. However, the optimal number is probably dependent on the user's browser and hardware as well as the task to be performed.

Testing and Debugging Web Workers

Over the past 10 years, the tools for JavaScript debugging have gotten quite good. Firebug and Chrome Developer Tools both are first-rate debugging tools that can be used for testing JavaScript applications. Unfortunately, neither one can access code running in a Web Worker. So you can't set break points or step through your code in a worker. Nor do workers show up in the list of loaded scripts that appear in the respective script tags of Firebug and Chrome. Nor can Selenium or QUnit directly test code running in a Web Worker.

Errors in a worker are reported back to the console in Firefox and Chrome. Of course, in many cases, knowing the line and file where the error occurred does not help all that much, as the actual bug was somewhere else.

Chrome does provide the programmer a method for debugging Web Workers. The Chrome Developer Tools script panel contains a Web Workers checkbox. This option causes Chrome to simulate a worker using an iframe.

A Pattern for Reuse of Multithread Processing

Being able to use Web Workers to pull complex functions out of the user's browser task offers great power for the programmer. Firefox has supported Web Workers since version 3.5 and Chrome has supported them since version 4. Safari and Opera have also supported them for some time. However, as of this writing, Microsoft Internet Exporer does not support Web Workers (though support may appear in IE version 10), nor does Safari on iOS, so it is not possible to use Web Workers on the iPad/iPod/iPhone platform.

What would be ideal is a library that would enable a programmer to abstract out the code to be run into a function or module and a runner that would use the best available mechanism to run that code in the backround: via a Web Worker if available, and otherwise via a `setTimeout` method. Furthermore, the library would provide a common set of interfaces that could be used for the various interactions, such as posting a message back to the main application.

Such a library should always use feature detection rather than browser detection to figure out which version of the code to run. While a given browser may or may not support Web Workers right now, in the future that will change and a library needs to be able to work with those changes.

The actual function to do the work in this pattern will be called repeatedly with the run state as a parameter. It should do whatever processing it needs to do and return a modified state parameter that will be used to call it again until it finishes its job and calls the `stop()` method, or is otherwise interrupted. The run function (see Example 8-6) should be treated as a pure function; it should just process its inputs and return a value, but not effect any change in global state, because a different set of interfaces will be available to it depending on whether it is running as a Web Worker or not.

Example 8-6. Run

```
(function ()
{
  runner.setup(function (state)
  {
    this.postMessage({state: state});
    return {
     time: state.time += 1
   };
```

```
  }, {
    time: 0
  });
}());
```

When running in a Web Worker (see Example 8-7), the run function can be run from inside a standard loop. The system is set up via a `postMessage` call with some initial parameters that are passed as the initial state to the run method. That method will be repeatedly called by the while loop until it calls the stop function, at which point the state will be posted back to the main message.

Example 8-7. Running a function with a Web Worker

```
var runner =
{
  stopFlag: false,

  postMessage: function (message)
  {
    self.postMessage(message);
  },

  stop: function ()
  {
    this.stopFlag = true;
  },

  error: function (error)
  {
    this.stopFlag = true;
  },

  setup: function (run)
  {
    this.run = run;
    var that = this;
    self.onmessage = function message(event)
    {
      that.execute(JSON.parse(event.data));
    };
  },

  execute: function (state)
  {
    var that = this;

    setTimeout(function runIterator()
    {
      that.state = that.run.apply(that, [that.state]);

      if (that.stopFlag)
      {
        that.postMessage(that.state);
      }
```

```
        else
        {
          that.execute();
        }
    }, 16);
  }
};

(function ()
{
  runner.setup(function (state)
  {
    var newstate = state;
    //modify newstate here
    return newstate;
  }, {
    time: 0
  });
}());
```

If Web Workers are not available in the browser, the method should be run through a short, repeating timeout instead of in a while loop (see Example 8-8). A while loop would block the message queue, so the main thread could not send messages to the worker. Using a timeout frees up the main thread—the whole goal of this library—and also lets a message change the state of the run function as needed.

Once again, the runner calls the run function with a state parameter that should be returned by the callback function. However, because this is not a Web Worker, the runner will then call the window.setTimeout() method to delay the next iteration by some amount of time and call the function again.

Example 8-8. Running a function without a Web Worker

```
var runner =
{
  stopFlag: false,
  // override this function
  onmessage: function (msg)
  {
    if (msg.state)
    {
      var state = msg.state;
      $('#status').html("time: " + state.time);
    }
    if (msg.set)
    {
      this.state = msg.set;
    }
    return this.state;
  },
  postMessage: function (message)
  {
    this.onmessage(message);
  },
```

```
  stop: function ()
  {
    this.stopFlag = true;
  },
  error: function (error)
  {
    this.stopFlag = true;
  },

  setup: function (run, state)
  {
    this.run = run;
    this.state = state;
    this.execute();
  },

  execute: function ()
  {
    var that = this;

    setTimeout(function runIterator()
    {
      that.state = that.run.apply(that, [that.state]);

      if (that.stopFlag)
      {
        that.postMessage(that.state);
      }
      else
      {
        that.execute();
      }
    }, 250);
  }
};
```

Communications between the simulated Web Worker and the main body of the code are also somewhat different. Because there is no postMessage() method with a callback, the runner must simulate it by presenting a mechanism to register a callback that can take the same parameters as the Web Worker's onmessage() handler.

This concept of how to make code portable between a Web Worker and regular Java-Script is presented as a model and not a full solution. It is missing some features, such as loading code. It is also missing a way to call an asynchronous method such as an Ajax call, and resume processing when done. This would be necessary because, although in general Web Workers are designed for processor-intensive work, there will be times when access to an Ajax call or IndexedDB makes sense.

Libraries for Web Workers

When programming JavaScript in the main thread, programmers use a library such as jQuery to improve the API and to hide differences between browsers. For use with Web Workers, there is a jQuery extension called jQuery Hive (*http://github.com/rwldrn/ jquery-hive*) that provides much of this functionality. Hive includes the PollenJS library in the main JavaScript thread. The library includes interfaces to create workers.

Hive will also encode and decode messages between the main thread and worker if needed. In some browsers (notably Firefox), complex data can be sent over the post Message() interface. However, in some versions of Chrome and Safari, postMessage() will handle only a string or other simple data.

Hive also includes a subset of the jQuery API in the worker itself. The most important methods in the Hive API are $.get() and $.post(), which mirror the APIs in jQuery. If a worker needs to access the server via Ajax, for instance, using Hive will make your life much easier.

Hive also includes access to a persistent storage interface via $.storage. To set a value, use $.storage(name, value). Calling $.storage(name) without the second value parameter will return the existing value, if set.

Also included in Hive are $.decode() and $.encode(), which can be used to decode or encode JSON messages.

CHAPTER 9

Web Sockets

HTTP is a request and response protocol. It was designed to request files and still operates around the idea of file requests. For the type of application that has to load data and then save it later, this works pretty well.

However, for an application that needs real-time data from the server, this works quite poorly. Many classes of applications require real-time or semi-real-time access to the server. Applications such as chat, or those that share data in real time like many of the Google Office applications, really need a way for the server to push data to the browser when things happen on the server. There are a few ways to do this with HTTP, but none of them really work well.

Some applications, such as Gmail, simply make a large sequence of HTTP requests, more than one per second, as shown in Figure 9-1. This has a lot of overhead and is not a particularly efficient way to poll the server. It can also create a huge amount of server load, as each request involves a setup and teardown that may need to happen on the server. Plus, there is the network overhead of HTTP headers, as well as user authentication. The HTTP headers can add a few hundred bytes to each request. In a busy server this can add a significant amount of load to the servers and network.

A second method is to open up an HTTP request to the server and let it hang open. When the server needs to send some data, it sends it to the client and then closes the HTTP request. At this point the browser will open up a new connection and repeat. Depending on the specific server technology employed, this can still cause a significant load on the server, as a large pool of threads and connections are kept running, even if in a waiting state, though this would be less of an issue using a nonblocking server such as *Node.js*. A further complication is that the browser may allow only a limited number of Ajax requests to a given server at a time, so holding a request or two open may cause other things to block, making this a less-than-optimal way to do things.

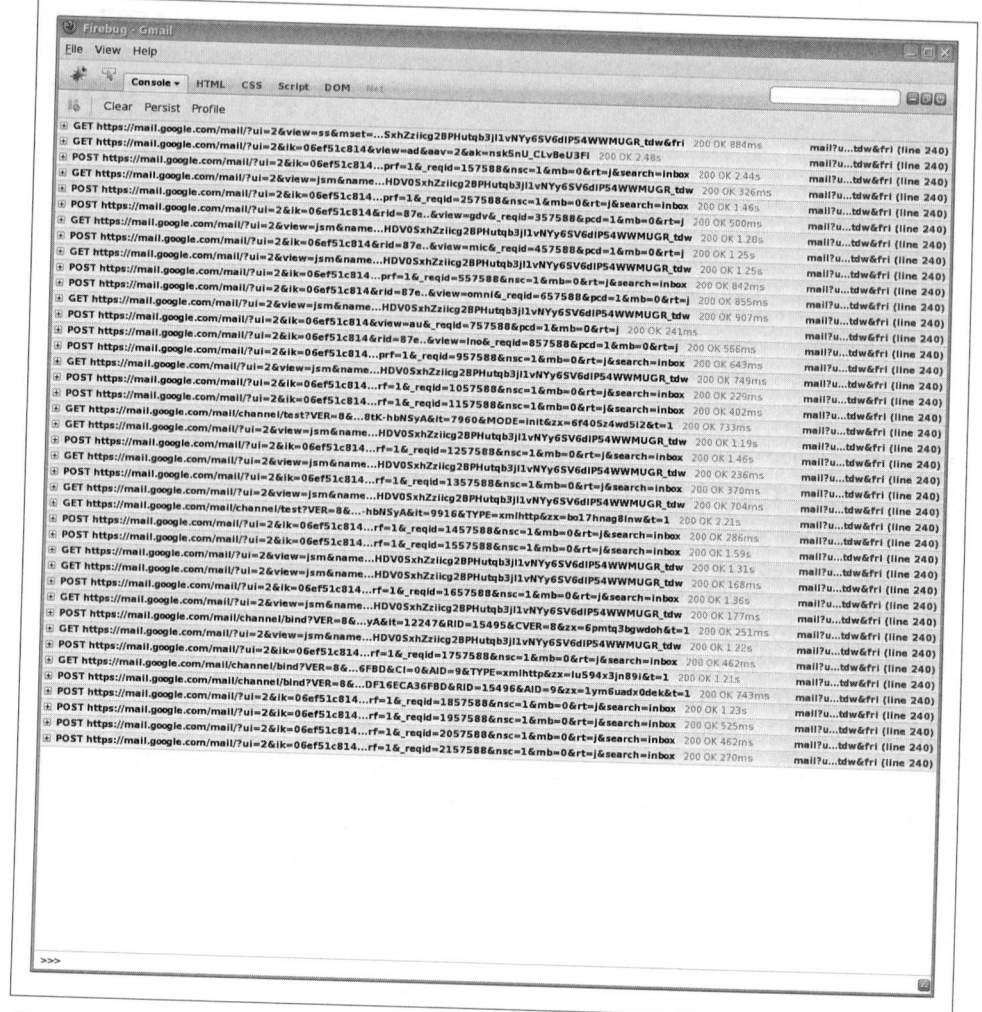

Figure 9-1. Firebug in Gmail

HTML5 introduces the idea of web sockets, which work a lot like classic TCP/IP sockets. A socket is opened by the browser back to the server from which it was loaded and can be kept open until it is no longer needed, whereupon it is explicitly closed. A socket is a bidirectional real-time data channel, while an HTTP request is a simple polling system. If you were to send each keystroke to the server over HTTP with Ajax, you would incur an overhead of 300–400 bytes at a minimum, maybe as much as a kilobyte or two with cookies, for each keystroke. A socket uses no HTTP headers, so much of that overhead will just go away. The overhead would be reduced to just a few bytes.

As of this writing (August 2011), web sockets are supported by Chrome version 8 and later and Safari version 5. As of Firefox version 6, web sockets are available, but the constructor is MozWebSockets. Opera has implemented the web sockets spec but leaves it turned off by default, pending work on security issues. For browsers that do not support web sockets, fallbacks using classic HTTP or Flash can work. There are also some libraries such as *socket.io* (*http://socket.io*) that will provide a constant interface for web sockets and the fallback to older-style HTTP communications for browsers that may not support web sockets. It is also possible to emulate web sockets via Flash for browsers that support Flash but not web sockets.

The Web Sockets specification document also appears to be a work in progress. While web sockets have been deployed in several browsers, there is still very little documentation on how to implement them. There have also been several earlier versions of the web sockets standard that are not always compatible.

The Web Sockets Interface

To use a web socket, start by creating a WebSocket object. As a parameter, pass a web socket URL. Unlike an HTTP URL, a web socket URL will start with ws or wss. The latter is a secure web socket that will use SSL, similar to HTTPS under Ajax:

```
var socket = new WebSocket("ws://example.com/socket");
```

Once a socket connection is opened, the socket's socket.onopen() callback will be called to let the program know that everything is ready. When the socket closes, the socket.onclose() method will be called. If the browser wishes to close the socket, it should call socket.close().

To send data over the socket, use the socket.send("data") method. Data is limited to strings, so if it's more complex, you need to encode it to JSON, XML, or some other data interchange format. In addition, sockets are text-only, so if binary data must be sent it should be encoded into text through some method.

Setting Up a Web Socket

A web socket connection starts out much like an HTTP connection. It opens a connection on port 80 (ws) or 443 (wss) to the server. In addition to the standard HTTP headers, it also includes some new headers that tell the server that this is a web socket connection and not an HTTP connection. It also includes some handshaking bytes to provide some security. Since the WebSocket protocol uses ports 80 and 443, most proxies and firewalls should deal with it correctly. Web sockets can also specify a different port in the same way that an HTTP protocol can, but like an Ajax call, the web socket must be on the same port as the web server that spawned it.

Once a connection is set up, both ends can send data over it. Any valid UTF-8 string can be sent. It is up to the server and the client to agree on a data format. Normally, data will probably be JSON or XML, but there is no reason that some other format could not be used if desired.

Web Socket Example

To illustrate web sockets, consider Example 9-1. Here a very simple JavaScript function opens up a socket to a server that serves up stock prices. The JavaScript sends a stock ticker symbol that it is interested in (IBM). The server will find a price for that stock and send it back to the client as JSON. The server could be set up to poll every five seconds for a new price and send it to the client when it changes. The client will just refresh the element every time the price changes.

Example 9-1. Socket client example

```
$(function ()
{
  var socket = new WebSocket('ws://localhost/stockprice');

  // wait for socket to open
  socket.onopen = function ()
  {
    socket.send(JSON.stringify(
    {
      ticker: "ibm"
    }));
  };

  socket.onmessage = function (msg)
  {
    var prices = $.parseJSON(msg.data);
    var html = "IBM: " + prices.ibm;
    $('div.prices').html(html);
  }
});
```

The browser code for working with web sockets should look pretty familiar to any programmer who has worked with Ajax. A web socket object is created with the appropriate URL. Once the socket is opened (be sure to wait for it to open), data can be sent via the `socket.send` event to the server. When the server sends data back to the browser, the `socket.onmessage` event is called with the string in the data field of the event object. In this case, the data is in JSON, so it can be parsed with the standard browser JSON parsing methods and then displayed in the browser.

The web socket client does not make much sense without a server to go with it. In general, web sockets lend themselves well to event-driven data such as a shared document, stock ticker, or chat service. Although PHP has often been the standby of web server development, in this case having a language with a programming model set up for long-running processes and events makes more sense.

There are several good choices here. Node.js works well, and has the advantage of being JavaScript, which the web programmer will already be familiar with. Other possibilities include Erlang and Yaws, which have a web socket interface and a multiprocessor model that could be ideal for this kind of programming. There are also a number of options for Java and the other languages based on the JVM, including Scala and Clojure. In addition, there are implementations for Ruby and probably most of the .NET/CLR languages. Most languages that are used for web server programming will be able to use web sockets.

In the following example of server code, done in Node.js (see Example 9-2), a server is set up using the `websocket-server` package, which can be found via NPM or on GitHub. The server waits for a connection on port 8080, and when one comes in, it calls the callback. That connection callback waits for a message to arrive via the connection object. In this example, it then calls a function called `tickerUpdate`, which somehow finds stock prices. When the relevant stock symbol has changed, the server invokes the callback, which sends the new price back to the client. For a more complete guide to programming Node.js, see *Node: Up and Running* by Tom Hughes-Croucher (O'Reilly).

Example 9-2. Socket server example

```
var ws = require("websocket-server");

var server = ws.createServer();

server.addListener("connection", function (connection)
{
  connection.addListener("message", function (msg)
  {
    var tickerSymbol = msg.ticker;
    tickerUpdate(tickerSymbol, function (price)
    {
      var msg =
      {
      };
      msg[tickerSymbol] = price;
      server.send(connection.id, JSON.stringify(msg));
    });
  });
});

server.listen(8080);
```

Web Socket Protocol

Most of the time, the low-level details of web sockets will not be of great concern to the programmer. The interfaces in the browser and on the server will take care of the details and just provide an API that can send data.

That being said, sometimes it may be useful to know the low-level details of how things operate, to understand why something is not working, or to implement a web socket client in some other environment. In particular, it is important to understand how a socket is set up.

Web sockets carry data between browser and server using a TCP socket instead of an HTTP envelope. When the browser tries to open a socket, it sends what looks like an HTTP GET request but with a few extra headers (see Example 9-3).

Example 9-3. Socket headers

```
GET /socket HTTP/1.1
Upgrade: WebSocket
Connection: Upgrade
Origin: http://www.test.com
Host: www.test.com
Content-Length: 0
```

After the connection has been set up, frames of data are sent back and forth. Each frame is started with a null byte of 0x00 and ends with the 0xFF byte. Inside the envelope is data in UTF-8 format.

There are server-side implementations for web sockets that work with Python, Ruby, Erlang, Node.js, and Java, as well as other languages. The state of libraries for web sockets is advancing, and there are packages in various states of development for pretty much all the major languages used in web development. In general, the choice of a server-side web socket implementation will be dictated by the other needs of a project. So it makes sense to find the web sockets package for the environment that is being used by a given project.

Ruby Event Machine

Ruby's Event Machine also provides an ideal platform for working with web sockets, as the programmer is given an event-based interface from which a stream of data can be sent to the client. The EventMachine::WebSocket interface closely matches the interface in JavaScript. As in the client, the EventMachine interface has standard event handlers for onopen, onmessage, and onclose, as well as a ws.send method to send data back to the client.

Example 9-4 shows a very trivial "hello world" type of web socket interface in Ruby.

Example 9-4. Ruby Event Machine web socket handler

```ruby
require 'em-websocket'

EventMachine::WebSocket.start(:host => "0.0.0.0", :port => 8080) do |ws|
  ws.onopen    { ws.send "Hello Client!"}
  ws.onmessage { |msg| ws.send "Pong: #{msg}" }
  ws.onclose   { puts "WebSocket closed" }
end
```

Erlang Yaws

Erlang is a pretty rigorously functional language that was developed several decades ago for telephone switches and has found acceptance in many other areas where massive parallelism and strong robustness are desired. The language is concurrent, fault-tolerant, and very scalable. In recent years it has moved into the web space because all of the traits that make it useful in phone switches are very useful in a web server.

The Erlang Yaws web server also supports web sockets right out of the box. The documentation can be found at the Web Sockets in Yaws web page (*http://yaws.hyber .org/websockets.yaws*), along with code for a simple echo server.

Example 9-5. Erlang Yaws web socket handler

```erlang
out(A) ->
    case get_upgrade_header(A#arg.headers) of
    undefined ->
        {content, "text/plain", "You're not a web sockets client! Go away!"};
    "WebSocket" ->
        WebSocketOwner = spawn(fun() -> websocket_owner() end),
        {websocket, WebSocketOwner, passive}
    end.

websocket_owner() ->
    receive
    {ok, WebSocket} ->
        %% This is how we read messages (plural!!) from websockets on passive mode
        case yaws_api:websocket_receive(WebSocket) of
        {error,closed} ->
            io:format("The websocket got disconnected right from the start. "
                "This wasn't supposed to happen!!~n");
        {ok, Messages} ->
            case Messages of
            [<<"client-connected">>] ->
                yaws_api:websocket_setopts(WebSocket, [{active, true}]),
                echo_server(WebSocket);
            Other ->
                io:format("websocket_owner got: ~p. Terminating~n", [Other])
            end
        end;
    _ -> ok
    end.
```

```erlang
echo_server(WebSocket) ->
    receive
    {tcp, WebSocket, DataFrame} ->
        Data = yaws_api:websocket_unframe_data(DataFrame),
        io:format("Got data from Websocket: ~p~n", [Data]),
            yaws_api:websocket_send(WebSocket, Data),
            echo_server(WebSocket);
    {tcp_closed, WebSocket} ->
        io:format("Websocket closed. Terminating echo_server...~n");
    Any ->
        io:format("echo_server received msg:~p~n", [Any]),
        echo_server(WebSocket)
    end.

get_upgrade_header(#headers{other=L}) ->
    lists:foldl(fun({http_header,_,K0,_,V}, undefined) ->
                    K = case is_atom(K0) of
                            true ->
                                atom_to_list(K0);
                            false ->
                                K0
                        end,
                    case string:to_lower(K) of
                        "upgrade" ->
                            V;
                        _ ->
                            undefined
                    end;
                (_, Acc) ->
                    Acc
            end, undefined, L).
```

The code is obscure if you don't know Erlang's syntax, but the key point is that the client can send various combinations of arguments (such as a TCP connection, a web socket, and an argument containing data) and have each message handled correctly depending on the arguments sent.

CHAPTER 10

New Tags

In addition to a lot of new interfaces for working with data, HTML5 also introduces a number of new HTML tags that can be used in a web page to enhance the application developer's ability to put out a quality application.

Tags for Applications

A common task in any application is to give the user feedback on how far along a long-running task is. This lets the user know that her task is moving and that something didn't freeze up. It is possible to show a progress meter by using a few `<div>` elements and some custom CSS, but HTML5 standardizes the procedure and appearance through a new `<progress>` tag. As of this writing, the tag is supported in Firefox and Chrome. It offers two attributes to make it easy to visualize progress to the user: `value` to show the current value of the progress bar and `max` to show the maximum value.

In order to show a progress indication to users of legacy browsers, it is recommended that you include some form of text inside a `<span>` element inside the progress bar.

Example 10-1 shows the code for a progress bar at 20% completion. Example 6-4 shows how JavaScript can update the attributes as events in the program indicate progress. The progress bar can also be styled with CSS like any other HTML element.

Example 10-1. Progress indicator

```
<!DOCTYPE html>
<html>
  <head>
    <title>Progress</title>
  </head>
  <body>
    <progress value="20" max="100">
      <span>running</span>
    </progress>
  </body>
</html>
```

If the `<progress>` element can be used to show a running event, the `<meter>` element can be used to show a static value such as how full a disk is or how much money has been raised for a fundraising goal.

The `<meter>` tag can take a few parameters, including `min`, `max`, `low`, `high`, `optimum`, and `value`. All of these should be set to numeric values. The `min` and `max` values show the ends of the range of values, whereas the `value` attribute shows the current value. The `high`, `low`, and `optimum` parameters allow the tag to subsegment the range. Through CSS, you can style values for different parts of the ranges with different looks. A `<meter>` tag is shown in Example 10-2.

Like the `<progress>` tag, the `<meter>` tag should be wrapped around a `<span>` that can show the data to browsers that do not support this tag. Currently, Chrome supports this tag, as does Opera. Other browsers may follow at some point.

Example 10-2. Meter indicator

```
<!DOCTYPE html>
<html>
  <head>
    <title>Meter</title>
  </head>
  <body>
    <meter min="0" value="20" max="100">
      <span>20%</span>
    </meter>
  </body>
</html>
```

Accessibility Through WAI-ARIA

For people with physical disabilities, using a web app (or any other GUI application) can be quite challenging. For these users, HTML5 defines Accessible Rich Internet Applications. These are directed particularly at the vision-impaired (which may include people who for some reason still use a nongraphic browser). By adding attributes to tags in an application, you may help these users access the application's contents.

This section is not a full guide to making an accessible application, which could fill a book of its own. The basic idea of WAI-ARIA is that it adds semantic meaning to elements on the page that can be read by a screen reader to let a user who is vision-impaired have context for what is happening on a page. This sort of text has been supported for some time by the `alt` attribute on `<img>` tags and the `title` attribute on `<hr>` tags.

The most common attribute in WAI-ARIA is the `role` attribute. This provides context for elements. In HTML, tags such as `<span>` and `<li>` are used for many different things, from navigation to actual lists. By adding a `role` attribute, you can help the screen reader make sense of all of this. Example 10-3 shows an example of WAI-ARIA.

Example 10-3. WAI-ARIA

```
<!DOCTYPE html>
<html>
  <head>
    <title>Meter</title>
  </head>
  <body>
    <ul id="tree1"
        role="tree"
        tabindex="0"
        aria-labelledby="label_1">
      <li role="treeitem" tabindex="-1" aria-expanded="true">Fruits</li>
      <li role="group">
        <ul>
          <li role="treeitem" tabindex="-1">Oranges</li>
          <li role="treeitem" tabindex="-1">Pineapples</li>
          ...
        </ul>
      </li>
    </ul>
  </body>
</html>
```

Microdata

Sometimes it is useful to add machine-readable data to a set of HTML tags. For example, you can use this procedure in a template to encode data into a page that can later be read by JavaScript. To enable such procedures in a standardized way, HTML5 created the concept of *microdata*, which can be added to HTML5 tags.

Traditionally, HTML tags give data about how information should be formatted on-screen, but not about the data itself. A program can look at an <li> tag and know it is an item in a list, but not what kind of list. Is it a list of books for sale, or people who attended an event? By adding microdata it is possible to give context to that data, which can later be used programmatically.

In general, microdata tags will probably be used in web pages more than in applications, but applications that run as plug-ins to a page, or administer a page in other ways, may be called upon to use microdata. One can imagine an HTML5 application that serves as an administrative panel for a company's website and offers spaces where a sales manager could put in microdata tags that give items for sale a context for Google Search or for JavaScript programs from an external vendor that may be added to a web page.

In truth, microdata is pretty simple: just a few extra attributes with standardized names attached to HTML tags, and some interfaces to work with that data attribute.

To designate a section of a page that will use microdata, give the enclosing element an itemscope. The vocabulary for the microdata is defined by using the itemtype attribute with a URL that defines the vocabulary. Within that, data is tagged by marking the enclosing HTML tag with the `itemprop` attribute.

A number of predefined vocabularies can be found at *http://www.data-vocabulary .org*. These include specs for Events, Organizations, People, Products, Reviews, Review-Aggregates, Breadcrumbs, Offers, and Offer-Aggregates. Google will understand these syntaxes to enhance search results.

In theory there should be interfaces in the DOM to parse microdata, but as of this writing they are not ready yet and implementation can be spotty. Thankfully, microdata is just HTML attributes, so it can be easily parsed and processed with CSS selectors via the DOM interface or with jQuery.

New Form Types

HTML5 enhances the classic form that has been in HTML since the early 1990s with a bunch of new form types. Most of these are variations on the classic `<input type="text">` tag that has been in use since the beginning. These new form types provide some much-needed flexibility in the types of input a form can take, and the interface it provides.

In many cases, on a mobile device, changing the input type will also cause the device to put up a custom keyboard to enable the user to enter the right kind of data. For instance, if `type` is set to `number`, the device can put up a numeric keypad. For a type of `tel`, the device can put up a numeric keypad that looks a little different but is optimized for entering phone numbers. For a type of `email`, the keyboard will be a standard QWERTY keyboard but modified for the entry of email addresses.

One input type that is especially useful for smartphone applications is the `speech` input type: `<input type="text" x-webkit-speech/>`. The speech tag will take what the user said and translate it into text. My Android phone, for instance, has a Google Search widget that can search by voice. The speech tag still allows the user to type text normally as well. When the user speaks, the input will fire the `webkitspeechchange` event, which can be used to interact with the user.

> Be warned that for users who speak English with foreign or other non-standard accents, this tag may prove very difficult to use. Many of my Israeli and Russian coworkers find that these inputs are not very useful. It may also have limited support for languages other than English. So if your application's users speak, for example, Polish or Hebrew, the tag may or may not be useful.

HTML5 adds the ability for a form element to be required. If the `required` attribute is set and the element is blank, it can be styled in CSS with the `:invalid` selector.

To display a slider that allows the user to pick from a range of values, use the `range` type. Specify a `min` and `max` value as well as a starting value.

Other input types are pretty simple and mostly allow the programmer to specify what kind of data is expected, and have the browser mark a field as invalid if it is not correct. Table 10-1 shows some of the possible options.

Table 10-1. Form inputs

Type	Use	Notes
email	Email addresses	
date	Dates	Min and max can specify a range
time	Time of day	Min and max can specify a range
tel	Telephone numbers	Pattern to specify format via Regular Expression
color	Colors	Format like #BBBBBB
number	Numbers	Will show up and down arrows
search	Search	Min and max can specify a range

Audio and Video

HTML5 also provides new support for audio and video via the `<audio>` and `<video>` tags. These tags should be familiar to anyone who has used the HTML `<img>` tag in that the audio source or video source is set with the `src` attribute. Both can be set to display controls with the `controls` attribute. Audio and video can also be controlled with JavaScript and styled with CSS.

A full description of how to script HTML5 media is beyond the scope of this book, but can be found in *HTML5 Media* by Shelley Powers (O'Reilly).

Canvas and SVG

In addition to providing sound and video support, HTML5 provides support for building graphics in the browser with both Canvas and SVG. Classic HTML can display images, but Canvas and SVG can do much more.

SVG is an XML standard for Scalable Vector Graphics, which is to say that images created in SVG can be scaled and rotated and manipulated. In addition, each element in an SVG image is an element in the DOM. So it is possible to, say, create a circle in SVG that can have standard JavaScript event handlers attached to it. Elements in SVG can also be manipulated as parts of the DOM; elements can be added, removed, or changed directly with the DOM or with jQuery. SVG elements can also be styled with CSS like any other HTML element. SVG is covered in depth in other books, including *HTML5 Graphics with SVG & CSS3* by Kurt Cagle (O'Reilly).

Canvas was initially created by Apple for use with OS X and then moved into Safari; it has since moved into most of the other browsers. Canvas provides a 2D drawing surface on which the code can render images. This was used in "Web Worker Fractal Example" on page 90 to draw a Mandelbrot set, but its full power is much greater than that. For a full treatment, see *HTML5 Canvas* by Steve Fulton and Jeff Fulton.

In addition to the 2D canvas, a 3D canvas based on WebGL has started to be implemented in a number of browsers. For demos and a tutorial, look at the HTML5 Rocks tutorial at *http://www.html5rocks.com/en/tutorials/three/intro/*.

Geolocation

The World Wide Web is, by definition, worldwide, but there are many things on it that are local. If I am searching for a pizza place, I probably want one that is near where I am located. Geolocation lets the browser determine the user's location by one of several mechanisms. If GPS is available (as it is on many smartphones) it will use that to get a location that is probably accurate to a few meters. If there is no GPS access, the browser can try to use information from cell towers or WiFi hubs; these methods may not be as accurate but often are good enough. If the goal is to find a local pizza place, knowing the location to a few blocks is probably good enough. In most cases the Geolocation API will require the user to approve the request.

To get the user's position, call the `getCurrentPosition()` method with two callbacks, one for a successful location and one for an error. In the case that the browser was able to find the user's location, it will return with the latitude and longitude, altitude if it can figure it out, as well as an accuracy parameter. If there is an error it will return with one of several error conditions:

```
navigator.geolocation.getCurrentPosition(userLocationCallback, errorCallback);
```

New CSS

In additon to new JavaScript interfaces and new HTML tags, HTML5 also adds a bunch of new CSS selectors, including `:nth-child()` and `:first-child` as well as the CSS negation operator `:not()`, which can be used like `:not(.box)`. These should allow developers to have more control over presentation of their applications.

In addition to new selectors, HTML5 includes support for web fonts in CSS. It is now possible to define a new font in CSS and include a TrueType font file in the CSS to get a specific look.

HTML5 CSS also includes some other pretty cool features. It is possible to be more specific in text overflow, to set opacity of an object in the DOM, to set up text strokes, to specify color by HSL, and a lot more. Of course, like everything else in HTML5, not all of these capabilities are supported in all browsers.

JavaScript Tools You Should Know

JavaScript is a young language in many ways. Although it has been around for about 15 years, only recently has it been used for large-scale projects. So the tools to help programmers do robust, debuggable programming are still being developed. Here are a few you should strongly consider using.

JSLint

This is Douglas Crockford's JavaScript syntax checker. JSLint can test JavaScript code for all manner of possible problems. You can run JSLint from the website (*http://jslint.com*) or locally. There is a Drag and Drop widget in the Yahoo! widget set, and you can run it from the command line with Rhino (discussed later). A simple bash script will make this easy to run (see Example A-1). You can even hook JSLint into your editor.

If you use one tool for JavaScript, it should be this one. To understand why, read Crockford's *JavaScript: The Good Parts*. That book describes in detail why JSLint makes the choices it does. It will catch many very common JavaScript bugs and should be considered a key part of every JavaScript programmer's tool set.

To configure JSLint on a per-file basis, you can put comments at the top of the file. These can turn options on or off in the file as well as tell JSLint about global variables that are defined elsewhere.

Example A-1. JSLint shell wrapper

```
#!/bin/bash

java -jar ~/bin/rhino/js.jar ~/bin/jslint.js $1
```

JSMin

It's a fact of life for JavaScript programmers that our programs are downloaded in source form to the user's web browser. This can be done more quickly through minification. JSMin performs a number of actions on a file, such as removing comments and whitespace. After running JSMin, files generally are about 30% of their original size. This means many fewer bytes have to be transmitted to the client.

 JSMin is a one-way process, so make sure you have a copy of your files around. It also should not be used in development, as it makes debugging very difficult. And before running JSMin, make sure to run JSLint.

JSBeautifier

If your JavaScript code tends to get messy, JSBeautifier (*http://jsbeautifier.org*) is a good tool to know about. It takes a JavaScript file and reformats it according to some basic rules. You can run this from the website or using Rhino from a command line on your desktop. All the JavaScript code in this book was formatted with this tool.

JSBeautifier can take a number of command-line options to specify indentation style and bracket style. Indentation can be tabs or spaces. The -i option controls indentation level.

JSBeautifier can also format JSON strings. Since it is written in JavaScript, you can embed it in other JavaScript programs. If you need to display a JSON structure at some point to a user, you can use this library to pretty-print it (see Example A-2).

Example A-2. JavaScript pretty printer

```
    #!/bin/bash

cp $1 $1.bak
export WORKING_DIR=`pwd`
cd    ~/bin/js-beautify

java -jar ~/bin/rhino/js.jar  beautify-cl.js -d ~/bin/js-beautify/ \
-i 1 -b -p -n $WORKING_DIR/$1 > /tmp/$1

mv /tmp/$1 $WORKING_DIR/$1
```

Emacs JS2 mode

Emacs JS2 mode (*http://code.google.com/p/js2-mode/*) is a very nice framework for JavaScript editing. For those who already live in Emacs, this is very helpful.

Aptana

For those who wish to have a full IDE to develop JavaScript in, Aptana (*http://www .aptana.com*) is a good choice. Aptana is a version of Eclipse customized for Java-Script. It has a lot of options that can be customized.

 Aptana will reformat code, but it sometimes does so in strange ways—not bad, so much as just a little different.

YSlow

In a large web application, it is not unusual for loading to go slowly. If this is happening, you can use YSlow (*http://developer.yahoo.com/yslow/*) along with Firebug to find out where the bottlenecks are. The tool goes along with *High Performance Web Sites* by Steve Souders (O'Reilly), who also created YSlow. It covers much more than JavaScript, because it shows when each file is transmitted as part of the web page.

FireRainbow

FireRainbow (*http://firerainbow.binaryage.com/*) is a Firebug plug-in that colorizes JavaScript in the Firebug script tab. It's a very nice way to make code a little easier to read in the debugger.

Speed Tracer

Speed Tracer (*http://code.google.com/webtoolkit/speedtracer/*) is a Google Chrome plug-in that lets you know what the browser is spending time on. Before you spend a few days optimizing JavaScript, find out if it will actually help. If CSS is the real bottleneck, this will tell you!

CoffeeScript

CoffeeScript (*http://jashkenas.github.com/coffee-script/*) is a cool new language that uses JavaScript as a compile target. If you like functional programming, this should interest you. It has been getting a solid following of late. There are several Coffee-Script books out or in the works. CoffeeScript claims to produce code that will always pass JSLint validation.

ClojureScript

If you like Lisp, check out ClojureScript (*https://github.com/clojure/clojurescript*), which is a compiler that will compile the Clojure dialect of Lisp into JavaScript. It comes from Rich Hickey, who created Clojure.

Rhino

Rhino (*http://www.mozilla.org/rhino/*) is a Java-based JavaScript implementation. If you want to build tools to run on a command line in JavaScript, this is the tool for the job. A number of JavaScript programs, such as JSLint, will run under Rhino as well as the browser. In addition, Rhino can be used to allow JavaScript to script Java objects, which can be pretty useful.

Node.js

Node.js (*http://nodejs.org*) is a new server-side platform under development as of this writing. It uses the JavaScript event loop to create a nonblocking server that can handle a great number of requests very efficiently. Watch this project for cool things in the future.

Index

We'd like to hear your suggestions for improving our indexes. Send email to *index@oreilly.com*.

C

C-type languages, 10
cache control headers, 79, 82
cache() method, 19
Cagle, Kurt, 115
callbacks, 8, 10
  alternatives to for loops, 23
  button, 30
  closures to construct, 11
  cursor, 65
  on DOM elements, 29
  from ports, 107
  and Web Workers, 100
  write, 66
  XHMLHttpRequest, 70
Canvas, 87, 91
<canvas> tag, 87
changes, storing, 57
chat applications, 103
checksum, manifest, 77
Chrome, Google, 4
  BlobBuilder support, 68
  debugging web workers in, 96
  Dev tools, 12, 51, 96
  filesystem access, 73
  IndexedDB in, 61
  list of closed variables, 12
  manifest list, 80
  postMessage() in, 100
  <progress> tag support, 111
  Speed Tracer, 119
  storage viewer, 52, 80
  web socket support, 105
  web worker support in, 97
Church, Alonzo, 10
click command (Selenium), 37
client-side data storage, 50
Clojure, 107
ClojureScript, 119
close() method, 89, 105
closures, 8, 11–12, 23, 63
cloud test farms, 42
CoffeeScript, 119
color form input, 115
composite functions, 13
config files, web server, 76
confirm() method, 9
content delivery network, 75
controls attribute, 115

cookies, 51, 54, 104
CouchDB, 61
Cranley, Ronan, 4
createObjectURL() method, 68
Crockford, Douglas, 4, 7, 117
cross-platform web development, 3
CruiseControl, 43
currying, 21

D

data record example, 62
data storage, 1, 49–59
data trees, 26
databases, 63
  adding and updating records, 64
  deleting data from, 66
  IndexedDB, 1, 61–66
  retrieving data from, 65
  SQLite, 50
DataStore object (Ajax), 8
date form input, 115
dblclick command (Selenium), 37
debugging
  Firebug, 4, 9
  and JSMin, 118
  manifest files, 81
  and Web Workers, 87, 96
$.decode() method (Hive API), 101
decoratedFib(), 19
deepEqual() method, 32
defer() method, 56
degradation, handling, 27
deleteEach() method, 66
doConditionalLoad() method, 56
DOM (Document Object Model), 1, 2, 29
downloading events, 79
Drag and Drop widget, 117
drag-and-drop, 35, 67, 71
Dragonfly, Opera, 4, 97
drop event (DOM), 71
drop handler example, 69
drop zone example, 71
DSt library, 58

E

Eclipse, 118
ECMAScript objects, 89
Emacs JS2 mode, 118

H

handleButtonClick() function, 30
Haskell, 21
Head First jQuery (Benedetti & Cranley), 4
Hello World testing example, 43
Hickey, Rich, 119
High Performance JavaScript (Zakas), 7
High Performance Web Sites (Souders), 119
higher order functions, 14
hoisting, 9
<hr> tag, 112
HTML 5
   Canvas, 87, 91, 115
   manifest declaration example, 76
   new CSS features, 116
   new form types, 114
   new tags, 111–116
   progress bar, 73
HTML5 Canvas (Fulton & Fulton), 87, 116
HTML5 Graphics with SVG & CSS3 (Cagle), 115
HTML5 Media (Powers), 115
HTML5 Rocks tutorial, 116
HTTP (Hypertext Transfer Protocol), 2, 103–110

I

I/O, 7
IDs, importance of assigning, 33
if statement, 9
images
   appending to documents, 69
   and Canvas, 87
   editing, 73, 87
   missing, 81
   progressive drawing, 94
   scaling example, 15
   streaming video, 73
   SVG, 115
   use of src attribute, 68, 87
   user access to, 71
<img> tag, 87, 112
importScripts() method, 89
independent event loops, 86
index() method, 65
IndexedDB, 1, 61–66
indexes, adding/removing, 65
indexOf() method, 16

info() method, 91
inner functions, 11
integration testing, 28, 34
interceptor methods, 18
Internet Explorer (IE), Microsoft, 22, 61, 97
iOS Selenium, testing applications for, 47
iPad/iPod/iPhone platform, 47, 97
isDuplicate() method, 66
isElementPresent() method (Selenese API), 44
isTextPresent() method (Selenese API), 44
itemprop attribute, 114
itemscope attribute, 113
itemtype attribute, 113

J

JavaScript
   array iteration operations, 22–26
   closures, 11
   currying and object parameters, 21
   expanding functions, 18–21
   expanding objects, 16–18
   extending objects, 25
   function statement and function expression, 9
   functional programming in, 13–16
   functions act as data in, 10
   helpful tools for, 117–119
   libraries, 4
   nonblocking I/O and callbacks, 7
   passing objects in Firefox, 89
   primitives in, 16
   prototypes, 16–21
   recent improvements in, 4
   runtime event loop, 85
   runtime model, 29
   syntax checker, 117
JavaScript Patterns (Stefanov), 7
JavaScript: The Definitive Guide (Flanagan), 7
JavaScript: The Good Parts (Crockford), 4, 7, 117
jQuery
   DSt plug-in, 58
   Hive extension, 101
   IndexedDB plug-in, 62–64
   jStore plug-in, 59
   library, 4, 15
jQuery Cookbook (Lindley), 4
JS2 mode, Emacs, 118
JSBeautifier, 118

About the Author

Zachary Kessin has been working on developing interactive web applications since 1994. In the past few years, Zachary's focus has been on building complex applications in the browser with JavaScript, browser-based testing with Selenium, functional programming, and code generation.

Colophon

The animal on the cover of *Programming HTML5 Applications* is the European storm petrel (*Hydrobates pelagicus*), also known as a stormy petrel. The name "petrel" is derived from Saint Peter, because the birds appear to walk across water—in reality, they are fluttering and pattering their feet just above the surface while looking for a meal. They are commonly found in flocks in the Atlantic Ocean and Mediterranean Sea, following ships to eat discarded food and even to take shelter on board in bad weather.

Storm petrels are the smallest European seabird, at about 15–16 cm in length with a 38–42 cm wingspan. Their plumage is primarily black, with a white rump and white coverts on the underside of their wings. Their beaks are thin and hooked, with a tubular nostril on the upper beak used to expel excess salt after drinking seawater. They have webbed feet and are able to swim, though they do not often dive for food, preferring to skim the surface of the water. The petrel's diet consists largely of small fish, squid, plankton, and crustaceans, as well as offal left by fishing boats and other shipping traffic.

The storm petrel spends most of its life at sea, only coming to land for breeding season. In large colonies, the birds build nests on inaccessible rocky coasts and islands around the north Atlantic and western Mediterranean. During this time they are strictly nocturnal, to avoid predation from larger seabirds like gulls and skuas. They only lay one egg each season. In the winter months, they migrate to the oceans off of western and southern Africa.

Many 18th- and 19th-century sailors called storm petrels "Mother Carey's chickens," and believed the birds were the souls of dead seamen that warned of oncoming storms. Mother Carey is a supernatural figure who was said to live on an iceberg in the north and was thought responsible for storms at sea.

The cover image is from *Cassell's Natural History*. The cover font is Adobe ITC Garamond. The text font is Linotype Birka; the heading font is Adobe Myriad Condensed; and the code font is LucasFont's TheSansMonoCondensed.

Get even more for your money.

Join the O'Reilly Community, and register the O'Reilly books you own. It's free, and you'll get:

- $4.99 ebook upgrade offer
- 40% upgrade offer on O'Reilly print books
- Membership discounts on books and events
- Free lifetime updates to ebooks and videos
- Multiple ebook formats, DRM FREE
- Participation in the O'Reilly community
- Newsletters
- Account management
- 100% Satisfaction Guarantee

Signing up is easy:

1. Go to: oreilly.com/go/register
2. Create an O'Reilly login.
3. Provide your address.
4. Register your books.

Note: English-language books only

To order books online:
oreilly.com/store

For questions about products or an order:
orders@oreilly.com

To sign up to get topic-specific email announcements and/or news about upcoming books, conferences, special offers, and new technologies:
elists@oreilly.com

For technical questions about book content:
booktech@oreilly.com

To submit new book proposals to our editors:
proposals@oreilly.com

O'Reilly books are available in multiple DRM-free ebook formats. For more information:
oreilly.com/ebooks

O'REILLY®

Spreading the knowledge of innovators

oreilly.com

Have it your way.

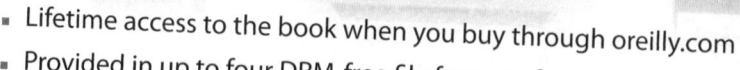